DARE

TO

How to
grow your
business
gracefully

SCALE

Warsha Joshi

AND

Evan Le Clus

Dare to Scale

First published in 2021 by

Panoma Press Ltd
48 St Vincent Drive, St Albans, Herts, AL1 5SJ, UK
info@panomapress.com
www.panomapress.com

Book layout by Neil Coe.

978-1-784529-37-6

The right of Warsha Joshi and Evan Le Clus to be identified as the authors of this work has been asserted in accordance with sections 77 and 78 of the Copyright, Designs and Patents Act 1988.

A CIP catalogue record for this book is available from the British Library.

This book is available online and in bookstores.

Contents

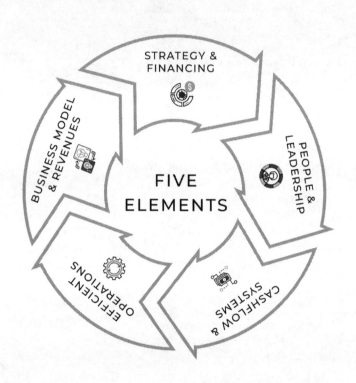

STRATEGY &
FINANCING

PEOPLE &
LEADERSHIP

CASHFLOW &
SYSTEMS

EFFICIENT
OPERATIONS

BUSINESS MODEL
& REVENUES

FIVE
ELEMENTS

CHAPTER 1

DARE TO TRANSFORM FROM FOUNDER TO LEADER

Dare to rise

You are here because you dare. DARE to dream big. You are here because you have the ambition to grow, transform and write your own history. Welcome!

The fact is you know it takes courage to stand up and be counted. If you have always been in a business family, courage to take up the reins. If you have been in the corporate world, courage to dream big and step out to start your own business. If you are a serial entrepreneur, courage to step in the craziness of creating a new startup! You may not have thought about this, but you may be imagining what your future self looks like and are taking steps to make that happen.

Well done for picking up this book and continuing to pursue the dream.

We mentioned writing your own history. Most of us work hard and in most cases to help someone else with their dream. The point is we all work towards somebody's dream and you, the entrepreneur, choose to work for your own. You pluck up the courage to stand strong for yourself to make a difference for those around you. Through your business you hold the power to transform the lives of your family, your friends, your business's stakeholders. Bring out the best in your team as you coach and mentor them, learn to manage your finances, develop your own leadership style, keep your investors and board happy as you grow your business.

And it is your dream that you keep front and centre that will keep you inspired long after everyone else has gone to bed.

Running your own business is one of the most exciting and rewarding things you can do. There may be times when you find yourself in the weeds, cannot see the wood for the trees and wonder what on earth you have got yourself into. The days seem to stretch and roll into one long and unending stream of task lists or firefighting.

A few years ago, we were having a conversation with Mira Johnson who was the founder of a children's nursery. She was going through a particularly challenging phase where the stress of establishing, operating and growing her business had begun to get the better of her. Mira had begun questioning the whole situation even to the point of second-guessing her own decisions. In situations like these it is common for owners to get their heads buried deep into the firefighting mode and somewhere lose sight of the dream which awoke the entrepreneur in them. During our conversation over a quarter closing session, we reminded Mira about her dream.

She, being a believer in the coaching process, closed her eyes, took a deep breath and placed herself on top of the mountain she had just climbed in her business to visualise her success. For Mira, this was a startling realisation of how the daily grind had moved her focus as a founder. This simple visualisation exercise has become her mantra to be practised whenever she feels overwhelmed. By doing this she found that she can recentre herself and focus on the right things in her strategy to move her business forward. Over the years, Mira's business and her own leadership style has left an indelible mark on her industry.

So, work with Mira here as you read her story. Take a deep breath and revisit your dream which led to your chosen business, the strength of your belief in the big vision you have now built based on that dream and importantly, the belief in yourself. Think about that dream for a moment along with the lessons you have learned from the challenges you faced head-on, the wins you have gained however big or small. Now feel the surge of energy flow in your veins, feel the goosebumps and the smile which has begun to appear on your face. You know that you have it in you, that you will find a way and you are not alone in this journey.

Welcome to the tribe that makes things happen, shapes the world and our futures. The tribe that takes on risks to touch and transform many people's lives. Families, teams, customers, suppliers, further outwards to their communities and beyond.

You may have wondered why we are writing this book. We have had the honour of working with some amazing founders who had very strong dreams and abilities but needed a guiding hand to get them on track. Over time we've noticed a theme or pattern where these founders, like Mira, had got stuck 'in' the business while losing sight of the fact that they needed to be working 'on' it. We often ask business owners why they went into business in the first place. Their answer is usually not too far from for freedom, for flexibility to create something which is their own to then nurture it to its fully scaled up version.

All answers lead to one destination which is to gain freedom from the proverbial 'rat-race' and that means working 'on' the business. Working as a team, Warsha and Evan come with a combined first-hand experience in business founding and operating and coaching expertise of over 50 years. We present to you our scaling-up perspective as you grow your business, whether you are only just starting out, you run an intergenerational family-run concern or are now the head of an established mid-sized enterprise.

We are writing this book to help you reconnect with your original big vision, trigger questions for self-awareness and to up the 'Scalability Quotient' of your business.

Scalability Quotient

So, let us take a quick detour to better understand the Scalability Quotient (SQ).

This is a 'Dare to Scale' assessment which gives you the 'SQ Score' for your business indicating how ready you are for rapid or high growth. The SQ score is based on five elements (the 'Five Elements') we look at when assessing a business's readiness to grow. Each element works in concert with the others and yet is identifiable as an independent area which can be honed to improve the overall effectiveness of your business. The Five Elements are:

- Business Model & Revenues
- Strategy & Financing
- People & Leadership
- Cashflow & Systems
- Efficient Operations

What we have built as a framework is an assessment which gives you an aggregate score to gauge your overall preparedness. It also gives you a score within each of the Five Elements. If you are reasonably strong in each of the Five Elements, you can begin scaling now with little disruption but if there are any weak areas it helps us zero in on them to implement necessary changes to lift your overall readiness score.

While each element might appear to be discrete within the overall framework of your business, they are all interrelated and can only work together. If there is one element that might have more weighting than the others it is strategy (closely supported by business model) in our opinion. By boosting your Five Elements and subsequently your SQ score you'll be in a great position to take on your 'ramp-up' goals.

Let's get back to where we were: more on SQ and the Five Elements later!

Know and live your company's transformational vision (your why)

So, let's go back to these wonderful founders whose success stories you will read throughout the book. Just like you did, along with Mira a few minutes ago, their first step to getting firmly back on track and to work 'on' their business was to reconnect with their dream. This dream on which their business was originally started stands on three strong pillars.

- The transformational vision
- Values

- Ethics

That is where we are headed now. Have a little scribbling pad and pen handy because you will need it throughout the book to jot down your 'light bulb' moments of clarity, your 'to-dos' and next steps.

As humans we collect experiences throughout our lives where we adapt to the best of our ability to make the most out of each situation. We learn along the way with every decision and action taken, creating our own individual stories of life.

When things are going great, we rarely look to improve. Something like: "If it ain't broke, don't fix it." We learn the most when things are not so great and we are challenged to put ourselves outside our comfort zone and into our 'learning zone' to find a solution. When we are paying attention, we are able to be at our creative best for the solution we seek. For most founders these learning zones turn into success stories leading the way to visualise the birth of their business whether it is to fill a need in the market or to make the most of an opportunity.

So, what is your story so far which makes you jump out of bed every morning and keeps you going throughout the day? This story is what we refer to as your own transformational vision.

While simple economic factors may have led you to start your business, you will find that your transformational vision is several layers higher than just to make money. Your dream could have been something like sharing a great product idea with the world, to build a business around a skill you are masterful at, a means to achieve your personal goals and dreams or even providing employment as your way of 'giving back'. Whatever your transformational vision, here we ask you to consider that when combined with your story, it creates your founder's DNA, which breathes life into your business.

Take Warsha's transformational vision for example, on why business coaching became her chosen path. The seed was planted during one of the biggest milestones in her life. She was born into a business family and while she was very young her father took over the family business from her grandfather (who passed on shortly after). As it happened, Warsha's father was more an academic than a businessman, ready to go to Oxford when he was pulled into the business. Bear in mind that this was in the late 1950s in India, where modern professional support systems like coaching, mentoring, guidance or even business peer groups who brainstorm for collective growth were unheard of. So, he did not have any means to gain the support or the guidance he needed and nor did he know who to turn to. Sorely lacking the skills to command the ship, the business eventually ran into the ground, breaking his spirit and consequently changing the course of Warsha's life forever. She was 16 years old then and the family had to start again.

Fortunately, Warsha's mother has an entrepreneurial streak and helped Warsha set up her first business which was the starting point in rebuilding the family's lives. Warsha went on to successfully found and exit three more businesses all the while learning on the job. Having lived through the initial extremely tumultuous entrepreneurial phase of her life, Warsha realised that every business owner out in the world should know that help is at hand, support is only a click away when they need it. Success would then hold a whole new meaning to these courageous men and women who have taken their place in the captain's chair. Warsha often says that her purpose is 'achieved' with each business owner she enables and empowers through her work as a coach.

You see, without purpose, each of us is just doing work and anyone can do that without risking too much. Contrast that with building a viable business where there is risk and responsibility but also, when you get it right, tremendous reward and success. It is important to remember the framing or the context of your decision to start and to vividly recall exactly how you felt with each win or success in your business. That feeling of success is key to understanding your 'why'.

The question to ask now is to see if your vision is still relevant today and are you in alignment with it? If yes, is it still the driving force behind the strategy, the brand positioning, brand promise and culture within the company? If it is not the driving force anymore then now is the time to set aside some quiet thinking time to see how that original vision has evolved. Some of the founders we have worked with used to write several versions of that evolving vision until one struck the right chord before working on realigning their strategy.

Know what your transformational vision is, be the founder who lives it and leads your company and your team by example.

You know that your vision is big enough and high enough when it transcends your day-to-day operational challenges! Keep this big vision in focus, wear your big picture thinking hat to build a robust strategy for laying the ground for your company's growth roadmap and chart your true course.

Living your vision means being able to successfully cascade the ethos of that vision throughout your company. Cascading it through to your team and departments, using it to develop and deliver your product to your customers to engage them along with all your stakeholders.

Importantly, conduct yourself as the inspiring leader that you are.

Remember, people buy from people they like and they will do so when they recognise a match with your vision and underlying values. View everything you do and everyone you interact with through the lens of your vision.

A true test of your vision is when you choose to work with customers, vendors and team members who are congruent with your vision, values and ethics. A true test of your vision is also when your vision, values and ethics show up in all areas, from your hiring process, your company culture through to vendor and customer relationships.

Values

Values are your set of principles which you stand by as a founder and choose to take into your business to support the vision. Before we go into a detailed discussion on them, take a couple of minutes to work with us on this grid to identify which values you hold dear.

Remember this list is a guide and you can add more values as you need.

Circle the top 10 values out of the grid. Choose those which you feel are most aligned with the way you view life, think, feel and live it, in no particular order.

Authenticity	Financial gain	Nature
Achievement	Fitness	Openness
Accomplishment	Freedom	Organisation
Adventure	Friendship	Partnership
Affection	Fun	Patience
Balance	Generosity	Peace
Beauty	Growth	Personal Growth
Challenge	Happiness	Perseverance

Change	Harmony	Recognition
Collaboration	Health	Reflection
Community	Helping others	Relationships
Compassion	Honesty	Reputation
Competence	Humour	Resilience
Competition	Inclusiveness	Respect
Connection	Independence	Safety
Completion	Influence	Security
Contribution	Innovation	Self-expression
Cooperation	Inspiration	Self-respect
Courage	Integrity	Serenity
Creativity	Intellect	Service
Decisiveness	Intimacy	Spirituality
Dependability	Intuition	Stability
Democracy	Joyfulness	Status
Diversity	Justice	Stewardship
Effectiveness	Knowledge	Teamwork
Efficiency	Laughter	Thoughtfulness
Enjoyment	Leadership	Tradition
Equality	Learning	Tranquillity
Ethical Practice	Legacy	Transformation
Excellence	Love	Transparency
Expertise	Loyalty	Trust
Fairness	Magic	Truth
Faith	Meaningful work	Uniqueness
Family	Money	

Now that you have your top 10 values, work with us through this quick four-step process to identify your top three.

- Think of these top 10 as the base of a mountain and as you climb the mountain, you go through a selection process to only take the ones which resonate with you the most. Only the ones which strengthen you the most.

- As you reach the first basecamp, narrow that list to the top seven.

- At the second basecamp, keep only the top five with you.

- In your final ascent to the summit bring only your top three with you.

Note your top three down and put them through a simple validation test: how fervently will you stand by them no matter the consequences from decisions based on these values? Feel free to go through the exercise again until you are certain you have the right set.

Now think of them when you next assess your strategy to see if and how strongly these top three values feature in it.

Why are values important?

When times are tough, we tend to avoid making hard decisions because we humans are inclined to take the path of least resistance. As a consequence, some of our values are the first casualties in our culture. If and when we allow that to happen, the message we are giving ourselves and all our stakeholders is that it is OK to alter our standards we had initially set. Standing by our values takes courage. By action (or inaction) we are showing what is negotiable or not. Remember to revisit your values identified above when we talk more about them along with ethics further in the book.

The transformational vision, values and ethics are the backbone of your company especially when they drive the strategy.

Your job is to set the direction

Now that we have talked a little bit about your transformational vision, underlying values and cascading them throughout your business, let's talk a little about your real role. As a founder, while you may be involved with day-to-day operations, remember to wear your big picture or strategic thinker's hat. The secret sauce to your success for your own transformation from a founder with a great idea to an inspired CEO scaling up your business is keeping your eyes firmly on the strategic big picture.

As founder and CEO, you must understand that you are wearing two distinct hats and you need to be very clear about which of those hats you are wearing at all times to ensure that the correct business priorities are under the spotlight. As a leader you must always transparently and consistently communicate your vision, values, and ethics to the team, ensuring you use all available communication channels so it does not just remain a 'corporate statement' that only pays lip service to the idea.

If you have a second in command already as your CEO, then they and your senior management team need to 'walk the talk' and behave in an observable way that is congruent with your culture. Without alignment to your vision, values and ethics, your business strategy, operations, remuneration, rewards and consequences will start showing cracks because the foundation is weak. Your CEO and your senior management team are your first followers and as the size of your company grows, they are the ones who make a bigger impact through the ranks than you do. How inspiring are you as a leader to your first followers, showing with your courage and strength what it is that you stand for?

Make living the vision, values and ethics fun. Engage the team by keeping it fresh and vibrant, mean what you say and say what you mean. If you become aware of a misalignment with your team, as CEO it is critical to be firm and take immediate action to underpin the culture and support the rest of the team.

Running a business is a team sport

Business, like any activity or sport in the world, needs a winning team to be led by an inspired founder. And remember your team stretches from your first team member through to your customers, suppliers, support system and family all working together to bring your vision to life.

Keeping your team together is easier that most of us think. Hire for culture fit first. It is important to hire the 'right' person who aligns with your company's culture rather than the other way round. Remember that upskilling is easier than working in alignment with the culture and the values it is built on.

Once you know you have the right hires, you want to delegate and trust your team to do their jobs. We all have different backgrounds and ideas, a healthy respect for each other and encouraging open discussion and debate of ideas goes a long way for your team to feel heard. Empower your team – delegate authority, not responsibility – so that you garner a strong sense of commitment which then allows for a strong culture of accountability. Accountability is further strengthened when you stand fully behind your team, no matter what. If you show deep loyalty to your people, they will totally stand by you too and give you more dedicated service than you can imagine.

You also need to be deeply attuned to your people, listening carefully and noticing everything. Always make room for town hall meetings where everyone hears the same information and you cull any rumours very quickly. Face hard facts, make tough decisions and follow through.

Whether we like it or not, there will be times when a 'bad egg' or some unhappiness finds its way into your team. By carefully paying attention you will have a head start on the matter and be able to nip it in the bud quickly.

It is best to address this head-on in a town hall meeting so there is nothing left in the unsaid. Handle the matter immediately, let nothing fester. Call out the matters and ask anyone who has an issue to speak up or hold their peace – be clear that undercurrents of dissent have no place in a transparent organisation. Let there be no elephant left wandering around your room!

Once you have your momentum in place, do set clear goals and expectations and measure your performance so you can fine tune your operations. Respect people for who they are and the experiences and perspectives they bring to the table. Encourage your team to own up to and learn from mistakes and most of all be human when learning from errors. Get this right and you find building a culture of accountability with a results-driven outlook becomes a breeze.

The courageous founder, you

You are here because you dare to take the step forward. Now, we dare you to scale even further. Begin your ascent. Conquer your mountain.

Dare to take the decision and get clarity in your vision.

Build a clear strategy towards the climb from knowing where the summit is, where the basecamps are along the way. As we go through the book, we will discuss how to choose your team wisely and surround yourself with equally inspired and aligned individuals with whom you will be scaling your mountain; from your coach, your climbing peer group who are on their own journeys to the summit, the team who will be taking on the responsibility of making this happen and the Sherpas or the frontline team who will be doing the heavy lifting for you.

Be the inspired founder to enrol your team in the transformational vision, values, ethics and the strategy. Set some consistent communication patterns between every division. Define each role, expectations of delivery and parameters of success, bearing in mind that delegation starts with you and when you do, trust your people to do what they do best.

Set the tone from the beginning by being ready to unlearn some of the methods, habits and processes of the past in preparation to train yourself to climb your mountain, training and coaching the team along the way. Likewise, in your business, smooth your path to scaling by checking everything from mapping your customer experience, service delivery, equipment or machinery upgrades to new and refined operational processes. Get everyone involved in bringing excellence in the execution of the strategy. Make operations efficient, precise and most importantly engaging and fun for everyone involved.

Just as when climbing a mountain, when you start scaling your journey, you will begin with tentative steps, there will be a few slips, a few falls and a few scrapes and bruises. Lean on your support system as they are always present to extend a hand and whisper confidence in your ear so that you turn around and do the same for your team. As you climb successfully, watch your confidence grow. The more confident you are, the more confident your team is!

Just like scaling a mountain, scaling your business successfully is immensely rewarding. It fills you with a great sense of achievement, with powerful confidence and fires up your ambition for the next mountain to conquer. Scaling successfully is one of the greatest teachers in life and business lessons. It is not for the faint-hearted.

Sir Winston Churchill famously said: "Fear is a reaction. Courage is a decision."

You are ready and we are in this together, so let's do this!

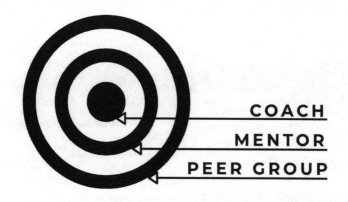

COACH

MENTOR

PEER GROUP

CHAPTER 2

DARE TO BUILD A ROBUST SUPPORT SYSTEM

You need a support system

You must have heard, if not experienced, a phenomenon which is often talked about in the entrepreneurial world. A lot of actual and virtual ink has been used in defining, analysing and brainstorming this phenomenon – from an individual or entrepreneurial community to a global perspective.

What is it, you ask? Well, we are talking about what every founder, CEO and for that matter, each one of us, in some aspects of our lives, experiences.

'Lonely at the Top.'

"It's sort of a lonely job," said Tim Cook, CEO of Apple Inc a few years after taking over the top job.

An alternative view on this is the feeling of being isolated instead of lonely; isolated because as the founder or the head of the business, you are probably the only person who can clearly see the summit you are shooting for. You are probably also the only person who is eating, breathing, sleeping and living the vision out at the front. As a founder you are the only person, at least initially, who is leading the various stakeholders of the company to success and who is ultimately accountable for the success or lack thereof of the business. As a founder and owner, you are the boss and at the top of your organisation. While that might sound great, it can lend itself to feeling alone and isolated.

By isolation we just mean there are times when you have tough questions and decisions that need to be taken and you will need someone to bounce ideas off. It also means that as head of the business you need to have a decent idea of what is happening in all areas of your business, from human resource matters, finance, your accounting, sales, marketing and your operations. It would probably be fair to say that you may not be an expert in all these areas and may need some help in order to take better decisions.

Sometimes we don't recognise isolation for what it is, and it can manifest as stress and can lead to your feeling overwhelmed and stuck in your entrepreneurial journey.

Let's simplify this a bit.

When you take up a new hobby, let's say it is hiking or mountain climbing, which no one else in your family or circle of friends is interested in, what do you do? Possibly research as much as you can through books, blogs, magazines and clubs. What comes next?

You might look for people in your area who share the same interest or look for online groups on hiking or mountain climbing. And since mountain climbing requires discipline, training, and dedication, you will in all probability look for a coach. Along with the coach you will find the experienced climbers stepping in as mentors at each level. Once you have found a group you have great chemistry with, you then look for people at your level to work together as peers to learn from, share ideas with, brainstorm, hold each other accountable and plan your next steps together. A beautiful mini ecosystem of support where everyone grows together.

As a leader you might believe that you need to be constantly adapting and learning. You probably do read a lot to keep up with industry and economic trends which help you with nutting out some of your issues.

Now, if you have chosen a good, strong second in command, while day-to-day operations may run quite smoothly, some strategic issues are best discussed away from the work team. So, who could you turn to for help? You might consider your spouse or family. You could get a consultant, but let's be frank here, you need to be doing the work. So, who else could you approach?

Sounds familiar? When you look carefully you will find that most successful people, particularly in disciplines like sports, the performing arts or business, usually surround themselves with like-minded individuals and thus overcome the feeling of isolation.

When immersed in this support ecosystem, you gain fresh and different views on challenges faced and how they are resolved. You also gain a place for constant development, where you can brainstorm, innovate, energise, inspire and be inspired.

What you need is a support system. Some fresh perspectives from like-minded people around you who will help you innovate, be a friend to your business and hold you accountable for some of the finer details and help you with the bigger picture.

There are three broad support systems you may consider:

- Coach
- Mentor
- Business peer group

The most common is to get a business coach to guide you. Other excellent choices are to get a mentor and to find a suitable business peer group to join. Underpinning each of these choices is a healthy debate of options around the issues, a genuine caring for your business and holding you accountable for your actions. If you said you would do it, make sure you do! This is important because your team may not have the courage to challenge you on what you say you will do. They will however notice if you fail to follow through and that could impact the tone you are setting from the top.

The power of the outside perspective of the three options does lift the bar and brings a lot of clarity to matters. Above all, this helps create a space for your advisors to speak to you at your level and will instil that all-important accountability for your actions. Opening yourself up to being held accountable will enable you to become more disciplined with your own commitments to the business and help you moderate your leadership style. Getting the right stuff done is the name of the game on your scaling journey.

So, which one do you go for? The simple answer is all three and we'll discuss why.

You need a coach:
Level 1, The Inner Circle

We will not be far from the truth when we say: "Behind every successful business leader is a successful coach."

When you hear the word coach, the first example you think of is usually sports, isn't it? The field of professional sports has harnessed the role of a coach like no other. Both aspiring and professional athletes recognise that having a coach enables them to break through boundaries, recognise weaknesses and build on their strengths. They help keep the focus and bring discipline into athletes' lives in order to successfully achieve superior levels of performance. Coaches will recognise the potential and play a significant role in helping enhance the skills of these athletes to take them to great heights.

Simply put, coaches are professionals whose primary focus is to unlock your potential and bring about results. They hold up the mirror so you can see what you often don't want to see, tell you what you would rather not hear and yet help you find that ray of sunshine by enabling you to find the answers on the path to success.

A close second to sports coaching, would you believe, is executive or CEO coaching. And why wouldn't it be the case? After all, professional sport is a business, and business is a professional sport. So why should coaching the founder, CXOs and every member of the team be any different? Most legendary business owners throughout history have had, and continue to work with, coaches.

Once, a long time ago, there lived a Zen Master. People would travel from far and wide to seek counsel from the wise Master, to learn from him the way of Zen. Kind and patient as the Master was, he made time for everyone who came to him. One of those visitors was a particularly successful businessman. He was a self-made man with an empire of which he was the founder. In his usual commanding and self-important tone, he said to the Master: "I have heard a lot about you and I have now come here so you can teach me about Zen. Enlighten me."

The Zen Master smiled and invited the businessman for a cup of tea. When the tea came, the Master, ever the servant, poured his visitor a cup. He poured and decided to keep pouring until his visitor said something. The tea got to the brim and the cup began to overflow. The visitor was stunned and yelled: "Enough. You are spilling the tea. Can you not see that the cup is full?"

With a knowing smile the Master stopped pouring and said to the visitor: "Can you see that you are like this cup? Full to the brim so nothing more can be added. If you want me to teach you something, first you must unlearn something and empty the cup. Come back to me with an open mind."

Emptying the cup or keeping an open mind are mindsets or ways of living which are easier said than done. It takes a great deal of courage to truly be in that zone. One person who lives this is Dhiren Bhatia, the founder of Cloudscape Technologies, who Warsha has been coach to for the past few years. The company offers cloud-based inventory management and point of sale solutions for the retail and the food and beverage sectors.

Dhiren comes from a family of entrepreneurs so starting a business was in his blood. He talks about his entrepreneurial mother and his parents opening a costume jewellery store.

He and his sister have fond memories of visiting the shop after school to help their parents manage their thriving business.

Later in life, Dhiren had a successful corporate career and decided to return home. Seeing a gap in the market for inventory management for retailers like his parents, Dhiren set up Cloudscape Technologies. Now as a second-time entrepreneur in a whole new region, Dhiren was on a steep learning curve and was beginning to get weighed down with decision fatigue. What should his business look like, the validity of his business model, who is his customer, how should the services be offered and good corporate governance were some of the areas he was looking to get clarity on. He even came close to wondering whether he should just close the business and return to the corporate world he was familiar with. He knew he needed help.

Dhiren started by tapping into his network for experience-based recommendations for a coach. While there is no 'one size fits all', the important things Dhiren was looking for was a certified business coach with a recognised pedigree and someone who could mentor him. Someone who would walk the path with him, help prioritise his approach from a holistic standpoint. A coach and mentor who would 'get him into shape' and enable him to see the wood for the trees.

You see, your journey with a coach starts with a discovery session where you and your potential coach will get to know each other a little and you will share where you are and where you think you might be stuck. This discovery session is as much for you as it is for your coach because you may be working with each other for many hours in the future and you each need to feel comfortable working together. What your coach is looking for in you is a willingness to make changes and to own that space, take bold steps and be that agent of inspiration and drive. Stated in a 'formula' you could say 'Mindset + Adaptability + Accountability = Coachability'. It is precisely this 'coachability' that you will need to have in you to make the impact you desire.

Let's talk a little about the 'formula'. Mindset in the scaling-up context is critical. It is about abundance, openness and sharing, being able to leave your ego at the door and be open to 'feed forward' (preferred over 'feedback' since it sets the intended direction more clearly). Having a mindset to be open to new ideas will naturally serve well in understanding and moving with our fast-paced world – remember that now 'smarts' (IQ) and maturity (EQ) are the expected norm – with the real value being how adaptable we are. How you are able to assess situations and see opportunity and plan steps to take.

Having decided you can work together, your coach will step into your circle and become a friend of your business while helping you. The coach will establish a subtle separation between your business and you so that you are able over time to work and think strategically *on* your business and not *in* it. The transformational vision you have set for the company will then be easier to implement and your own personal dreams and goals can then blossom in your personal space.

When you decide to work with a coach, a great deal of thought must go into choosing the right one to work with. There are a few things to bear in mind during the process. Assess what is important for you and consider what might be important for your coach when making the decision to work with you.

Some points to ponder:

For you:

- Where is your business at (what level of growth) and where is it that you want it to be?

- For what purpose are you looking for a business coach?

- What transformation would you like to see in yourself, your team and your business?

- Who along with you do you see the coach working with in your business (i.e. independently for personal breakthroughs and together with you occasionally for specific business matters)?

- How coachable are you and what limiting beliefs are you looking to break through?

- How do you prefer the coaching to take place (i.e. face-to-face and/or virtually)?

For your coach:

- Chemistry is key. Meet with the coach to explore alignment in mindset, values and business experience.

- Look for the coach's deep knowledge of running a business, their own mindset, adaptability, accountability and coachability. While specific industry knowledge of your business is useful, it is not essential.

- Ask for a discovery session. Further explore their alignment to your strategic vision, their strength and experience as a coach. You should ideally leave the session feeling inspired and empowered, filled with courage to take on your mountain ascent and ideally you would have, for example, say three action points to implement for you and/ or for your business.

- Take your time in identifying the right fit, because when you find that fit, your coach will become an invaluable part of your monthly routine and you will together build a strong partnership to take your business forward; a partnership which is built on the solid foundation of complete trust and honesty from both parties.

A great coach is an inspiring leader first. They build trust, confidence and respect with those they coach, they ask questions, encourage thought-provoking and stimulating conversations, they respect the team, they are business savvy and above all, they are results driven. As a 'coachee', surrender to the process with humility, allow yourself to be held accountable, face the hard facts, act swiftly and watch the magic happen.

What Dhiren said he found in his coach, Warsha, was someone who understood the pain, stress and uncertainty an entrepreneur faces, a skilled practitioner who helped him unlock his own potential as a creative entrepreneur, a friend who created a safe and confidential space to be able to work through his insecurities to come out a stronger person, a mentor to extend a helping hand. He found in her a coach who held him to task and accountable for his actions and yet guided him to get out of the weeds. Dhiren immersed himself into the process with an open mind, eager to learn, willing to adapt, daring to challenge and be challenged and continues to scale his business to great heights as a brilliant leader and runs a high-energy business that is so much more than just transactions.

One of the areas where Warsha likes to bring some distinction is for the coach to be able to separate the founder from the business. While she is essentially coaching the founder through to their full potential, Warsha also wears another hat, that of being a 'friend of the business' which enables her to see accurately if any decision being taken is for the good of the founder rather than the business (in other words she looks out for any 'secondary gain', or hidden agenda).

Needless to say, the coach and mentee partnership with Dhiren continues today.

Now back to your business.

In the spirit of professional sports being a business and your business being a professional sport, one of the critical things to bear in mind is that in both fields, your team comes first. While you are being coached to unlock your full potential as a founder, to transform into the inspiring leader for your team and turn the business into a healthy going concern, the secret sauce is in unlocking the full potential of your team. As a leader, make the team's success and wellbeing your biggest priority. A great coach helps you to build that strong culture of accountability within your organisation which we will explore together later in the book.

There will be some unlearning that needs to take place because it is true that 'what got you to your first million will not get you to your next five' (loosely paraphrasing Marshall Goldsmith: "What got you here won't get you there"). And this is precisely where the quality of 'coachability' comes to the fore. You will need to assess and refresh many if not all areas of your business including how you yourself engage and run it in order to establish the right footing and move forward at pace. Your coach will be there to encourage you, ask the right questions to keep your company's interests front and centre and to hold you accountable for your actions towards applying the necessary changes required for your scaling-up journey.

You need a mentor: Level 2, The Pioneers

To a founder, coaching and mentoring may seem to be the same or have a common thread with little distinction. Scratch the surface a little and you will find there is a world of difference to be observed. First and foremost a mentor is a subject matter expert and normally in a niche like marketing or finance, or alternatively could be a veteran in your industry. The mentor has already achieved considerable skill in the area (i.e. knows more on the subject than you do) and will come in to teach you about aspects of the subject where you have gaps. The mentor is not a consultant who does the work but is rather a guide and educator for you, and if tasking is given to you, will be your accountability buddy. While you will generally work with one business coach for a longer engagement, it is common to have more than one mentor, possibly for shorter timeframes, but who only focus on niche sections of your business.

The search for a suitable mentor would in all likelihood follow a broadly similar process as selecting a coach. You would need to establish where the gap is in your skill set and how important it is to address. If you already have a coach you might discuss this with them and seek a possible referral for you to approach. The important thing here is to take action to get yourself better informed so as to engage more fully with that area of your business. As with a coach, you would be looking for a mentor with a proven track record, someone with whom you have a strong rapport upon which to build a solid working relationship.

Mentors will come in different types and engagement styles, the most important distinction being professional or informal. The choice to pay for a service is ultimately yours but the decision should be based on what is best for your business. An informal mentor could be a family member with plenty of availability and skill set but you may find it's not structured enough and a poor fit. A professional setting has a better chance of setting appropriate boundaries and expectations and would also encompass follow-through on the accountability element.

Stan is a digital marketing professional who runs a small practice which was not yet large enough to warrant a dedicated bookkeeper, so he was also doing the books in the spare time he could find when not delivering the service to his clients. Stan used to be part of a networking group that Evan attends. Stan's strength was in his creative field and he reached out to Evan, the finance professional, for mentorship in the field. "Someone who could guide me to get the right things done and things done right," he said.

As with a coach, once you are happy with your choice of mentor you would follow a similar discovery period which is then followed up with regular sessions to achieve an agreed outcome. It could be as simple as understanding your financials better and updating dashboards with appropriate KPIs for your business. It could be a deeper dive into the world of digital marketing, crafting your own content and getting a better handle on converting organic traffic into sales more efficiently.

Whatever the area of focus, the key outcomes that you are achieving would naturally feed back into your inner circle with your coach (if you have one) to update your overall progress in your journey of growth.

Stan's practice is now a fully-fledged business and Evan is still his finance mentor.

You need a peer group: Level 3, The Advisors

The power of a peer group is one of the most underestimated of the three levels of the Support System.

As youngsters we sat together with our fellow students in school, in activities like Scouts and Guides, in pursuit of hobbies, in team sports, in playtime, etc. While we learned from our teachers, nearly every activity as a child was with friends who learned from each other. Warsha often remembers instances from school. As a Girl Guide, she was 'in knots' when learning to master the different types of knots and her friends simplified it for her because the aim was to succeed together as a group. Warsha remembers the ambition of a few in the group firing everyone up and soon they were joining hands to make sure everyone climbed the hill as one during many an outdoor lesson. As a result of the bonds formed in our journey to the same destination we stuck together as a group for years after that.

We, as humans, reach adulthood, pursue our occupations, start businesses and somehow forget that one of the best ways to learn is from our peers. As adults, we fear failure, we fear judgment especially from people close to us and in so many cases we continue to keep up a brave front in order not to worry our families and employees. As adults we begin a juggling act with things like bringing up our families, climbing the corporate ladder, setting up and scaling up our businesses, day-to-day firefighting in not just our businesses but lives as a whole. We bet you can add a few more items to this list!

This juggling act soon leads, without you even realising it, to you building an invisible wall around you that creates a bubble of isolation to cope with it all, leading to being 'lonely at the top'. For the purposes of this book, let us focus on the founder's challenges of running and scaling their business. The truth is you need to find a safe, confidential and harmonious space to talk, share your experience, learn from others' experience, brainstorm and find results-driven solutions, hold and be held accountable for your actions and goals. This support will keep the fire of ambition blazing to scale your mountain together.

The safe place you are looking for is quite simple really: peer groups, of course. There are many kinds of peer groups out there, and we'll discuss them shortly. When you are serious about building your support network for your business you will be looking for one that is structured, accountability based (results driven) and preferably coach-led (facilitated).

First let's take a step back and take a high-level view. If you zoom out to 40,000 feet and look at businesses in your industry, your suppliers, and other businesses around you, you may quickly get a sense that each business would have had similar challenges to you at some point. Remember too that every large corporate was once a startup, and even they had to learn and grow and evolve to where they are now. So, if it is true that you can recognise similar challenges then it follows that no challenge you are facing is unique. It's just that you have not found a solution yet and someone else ahead of you has. Similarly, you may have found a solution for one of your challenges, but the owner across the street may be grappling with it right now. And just as you did in your formative years, this is a perfect time to collaborate with fellow owners, like-minded in what you do, and with your experiences to back you up, work together for a common outcome which is to grow together.

You may have noticed large companies have boards and sub-committees and this is how they strategically support the CEO and management team. Your peer group, made up of like-minded entrepreneurs, would loosely work in a similar kind of way, where each member is mutually supporting the others, independently and for a shared purpose and experience. "It is an amazing experience to meet peers with whom we can share ideas in a safe environment" is a memorable quip from one of our own group members and this aspect alone banishes any sense of isolation or 'loneliness at the top'.

There are two principal types of peer groups – the formal and the informal/social. The informal/social are great forums for collegiate business owners to catch up over a coffee and discuss trends in the market, changes in customer behaviour or even new software platforms that help you run your business better. These kinds of groups are invaluable to keep in touch but may not consistently help with your business growth, particularly with takeaway action points and accountability.

By contrast a formal group has a clearer meeting structure and purpose, such as a regular brainstorm session of business owners implementing best practices through to a mentor grouping to implement a new tax. Tweak this kind of group and introduce a business coach to facilitate and you now add a whole new level to the power of a peer group. Group coaching and 'hand-holding' through application of growth concepts will give the entrepreneur a valuable learning space which, when you add accountability for action steps, is a powerful place to begin taking your business forward.

Underpinning any kind of peer group are six key principles you should look out for:

- Clearly defined common purpose

- Confidentiality

- Respect for each other

- Abundant 'can-do' mindsets

- Consistent structure in regular meetings

- A spirit of accountability that leaves egos at the door and challenges obfuscation (or 'BS' in simple terms)

Your time is valuable and it is worth taking a little extra effort to do your 'due diligence' on any group you are considering joining. Six months down the line you want to be in a position where a strong group rapport has been established, help is given and received effortlessly and you have found that place where you can talk about challenges and feel you have 'come home'.

There is a facet of a peer group that you may have heard of – it is also known as a 'mastermind'. The term was coined in the 1920s by Napoleon Hill and is most famously discussed in his book *Think and Grow Rich* where he discussed leveraging the potential of a mastermind. He gave a definition of a mastermind as: "The coordination of knowledge and effort, in a spirit of harmony, between two or more people, for the attainment of a definite purpose." The idea of a mastermind group is not a new concept and has been used by people from all walks of life for centuries. In relatively recent business contexts, such groups have been famously used by business icons who are now household names.

A notable mastermind group from about a century ago was called 'The Vagabonds', which you may have heard of. So, who were 'The Vagabonds', you ask? Well, they were people who revolutionised the world around them.

- Henry Ford, the automobile giant
- Thomas Edison, the famous scientist and inventor
- Harvey Firestone, the tyres and rubber mogul
- Warren G. Harding, 29th President of the United States
- Luther Burbank, the pioneering agricultural scientist

While these titans were hardly 'unsettled', 'The Vagabonds' were a powerful group. Each one of the 'vagabonds' was already on the path to achieving some of the most impactful things for the then emerging modern life.

So now imagine this. You have, as your trusted and constant core group, eight to 10 like-minded business owners who meet routinely. You meet for brainstorming, problem-solving, inspiring and learning from each other, and importantly, relentlessly holding each other accountable for taking action you have all committed to. Sounds great, doesn't it, to have a strong support system like this?

Surround yourself with like-minded people who share your vision, values and ethics. Bring about the alignment of these smart and creative heads by being part of a coach-led or facilitated peer group mastermind.

Dhiren, who you read about earlier, has built his full support system around him. A couple of years ago he joined his peer group mastermind. He shared his biggest takeaway after the very first meeting he attended. We still remember him saying: "…ten heads are better than one. This is a place to brainstorm and a place where my peers will hold up a mirror to me. Today I have experienced the full power of this space. I am in!" Dhiren continues to be a valuable member as he, along with his fellow members, dare to rise together and challenge each other.

Here's a fun question: do big names join a mastermind or do masterminds produce big names?

When you are building your business, especially when you are growing quickly and are in that scale-up phase, it is important you have a decent support system around you to bounce ideas off. We've discussed the three main support structures you can engage and where they sit in relation to you as the founder and CEO of your business.

- A business coach will bring some structured thinking to your space.

- A mentor will bring you focused learning and experience in a particular part of your business.

- A peer group will bring you diverse perspectives from other like-minded entrepreneurs around you whose experience you can draw on and apply to your own business.

Three different perspectives and yet one combined outcome which is the betterment of your business.

As we asked earlier, which do you need? The simple answer is all three for sure.

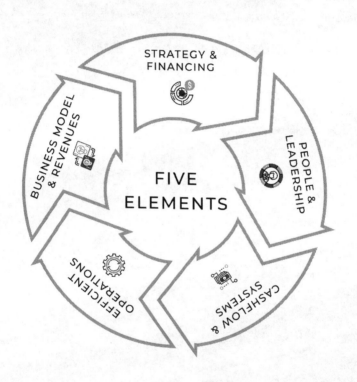

STRATEGY &
FINANCING

PEOPLE &
LEADERSHIP

CASHFLOW &
SYSTEMS

EFFICIENT
OPERATIONS

BUSINESS MODEL
& REVENUES

FIVE
ELEMENTS

CHAPTER 3

DARE TO LEARN TO RUN A BUSINESS

The foundations of your business

Evan remembers as a teenager watching his mum when she was running her business and thinking he 'got' it. He was, after all, studying accounting and business and it seemed pretty straightforward. His mum had a very busy and profitable general trading store with a handful of employees, so how hard could it be? Oh, the 'wisdom' of youth! What he did not see was there were a ton of nuances and levers that required attention that frankly he had no idea about and could only have ever seen if he had been more deeply involved.

Building your business is a team sport whether it be the team in your business or your support system.

Imagine playing a game of soccer alone and wondering why the other team thrashes you every time… a business is bigger than just one person. What Evan has since come to realise about his mum's business is that there is not enough time to do everything your vision requires by yourself – it requires duplication of yourself by gathering a team around you, and there are a number of fundamentals you need to take care of or the whole vehicle will implode.

There is a clear distinction between being self-employed and running a business and the clearest indicator of that is your time. There is a lovely quote from Gill Fielding that sums it up beautifully: "You become wealthy when you separate what you do with your time from what you do for your money," and with this perspective Evan now 'got' it, that it is your vehicle that will make you money, not you directly. If you can take time off from your business and find it does not directly rely on you to keep going, there is a good chance you are running a business rather than being self-employed.

Warsha's favourite anecdote is of two architects turned business owners. There was once a pair of successful architects who were at the top of their game at a renowned architectural firm. As a team they designed and built iconic buildings and were recognised throughout the region for their work. Ambitious as they were, a day came when they wondered what life would be like if they were to set up their own company. They wouldn't have to work for or report to someone, they would have the freedom and flexibility to express their creativity, to be independent.

So off they went from the firm and set up their own company. Their reputation preceded them and work continued to flow in. Slowly and surely things began changing as only then they realised that while they excelled at building buildings, they were on a steep learning curve to build and actually run their business! The skills required were vastly different from what they were good at and enjoyed doing.

The realisation setting in was that while it had its own challenges, when working at the established architectural firm they had the luxury of being part of a well-oiled machine which someone else had built and was looking after. Now as heads of their own company, they were being pulled in different directions which meant less and less time was spent building the buildings they were known for!

Something had to change.

Commonly we find that most business owners, while working in their business, identify themselves 'as the business' and therefore are unable to separate their personal goals and ambitions from the growth goals and needs for their business. You may also have heard founders refer to their business as 'their baby'. The minute we identify a business as our baby we are at risk of smothering the business and making ourselves a bottleneck that constrains the business from growing and flourishing. Remember that the business is an entity with its own independent and (for want of a better word) adult requirements which are very different from a baby's.

So, what are those needs that are specific to a business? These needs are grouped into the Five Elements we mentioned in the first chapter – the building blocks of your business:

Five Elements:

- Business Model & Revenues
- Strategy & Financing
- People & Leadership
- Systems & Cashflow
- Efficient Operations

Remember the SQ score? It is an overall scalability score for your business and is based on the assessment of each of your business's Five Elements. The stronger each element, the better, and in aggregate the better they work together, the stronger your SQ Score.

Element 1: Business Model & Revenues

Your business model is a high level and simple 'flowchart' of how you solve your customers' problems and how you make sales to generate cash inflows. Your detailed strategy that links your vision to your customer is discussed separately because keeping your business model simple can easily be overlooked when considering all the details of running your business. Evan recalls his mother's business where she started with £5 (serious bootstrapping!) and built on from there, but at every turn she was providing her customer with the best value for miles around on grocery and drapery items. Full stop. Very simple to articulate and easily referenced with each strategic decision being considered. Your business model is always the starting point of your journey and like Zig Ziglar said: "Nothing happens until something is sold."

As you build your business you will need to flex your business model to accommodate growth and after some time it could be that you may need to consider a secondary model. We were recently watching *The Founder* on a streaming service and loved how the McDonald brothers' story was told. The initial pain of customers was that burger shops in the early days were very slow and the product very inconsistent.

The McDonald brothers created their 'Speedee' system to produce food quickly and consistently so that customers could order and be on their way without delay with consistently high-quality food. The efficient process allowed the company to then set their pricing at a level that was very hard to match. This wonderfully simple combination of efficiency and scale in a restaurant is a powerful business model which is still at the heart of what McDonald's do but in the early days was a bottleneck to the company's expansion which later became a choke point which they controlled.

It became apparent that upholding quality standards was difficult to enforce with franchisees and that is where Ray

Kroc finessed the higher level corporate franchise and business model so McDonald's could ensure consistent restaurant product quality at scale. The film is a great watch if you have not seen it, and the rest is history, as they say.

Element 2: Strategy & Financing

Picking up straight after the discussion on your business model and revenue generation, we now step into the most creative of the business elements. Strategy and financing the strategy. An amalgamation of left-brain and right-brain thinking, abstract yet tangible, a thinking process which takes a deep dive into your business model and directs the actions to be taken.

You remember Dhiren, the founder of Cloudscape Technologies. As someone with a tech background, Dhiren has a great mind for product development while keeping a keen eye on the business model. The area where he needed the depth of knowledge and experience was in building the strategy for his new business.

When a new business is set up, the founder usually places most available resources into potential customer contact building with the aim to sell and deliver the product in order to begin generating revenue. Nothing wrong with that of course. Yet these are the very businesses which, when past their initial growth stages (hiring their third employee, around their 50th order or when entering their third year of operations), begin to realise that scaling up seems like an extremely arduous journey. Founders begin to experience the stress, days begin to feel like a grind and energy levels of the early days run low. In short, the word 'inspiration' feels a little worn out… and these are all symptoms of a lack of depth to their strategy.

As a coach, Warsha listens for clues in a founder's language like:

- "We are growing at a fast pace and yet are struggling to keep up."
- "We have happy customers yet our cashflow doesn't show it."
- "We have a skilled set of people working in the company and I am not sure if we all work together as a team yet."
- "We have a great product and yet we are struggling to set ourselves apart from the competition."
- "We are always so busy yet we never seem to get on top of things."

All these statements are clues that arrive at the same conclusion: there is a lack of a robust strategy which usually coincides with decision fatigue about how and where to invest cash to improve the situation. Most new businesses hit what we call a 'stress ceiling' and it's only then that they begin to delve into their detailed strategy. By the way, 'stress ceiling' is a strong indicator that the business may have a low SQ score and is not ready for rapid or high growth.

Your business strategy is the blueprint, the growth roadmap of your business. The second element in the foundation.

When you set your eyes on a mountain to conquer, the actual climb begins only after articulating why or the purpose which is driving the mission. Getting the right people together for the various roles, gathering the funds and equipment, assessing the rock face for the best path, training for the climb, are all subsequent tasks. Simply put, thinking through the process, planning and mapping out the destination before actually rolling up your sleeves to begin the work is the first step.

So, let's go back to Dhiren and pick up his journey. His business was just under a year old when he hit his 'stress ceiling'. In one of the initial discovery sessions, we tackled the strategy question and, needless to say, that is where we began: by taking a few steps back to take a few hundred forward. Work began on identifying the broad belts of strategy:

- The Why
- The What
- The Who
- The Where
- The How
- The How Much

Bear in mind that these are called 'broad belts' because each of these belts has several facets within it to work through in order to make sure the belts are tightened to create a sound strategy.

As we go along through the following chapters, we will continue to expand on these broad belts for you to work on them as well. Read on to see how Dhiren progressed!

Element 3: People & Leadership

Most of the life lessons we think we learn as adults are actually, as Warsha has noticed, merely refreshers, because some of the greatest lessons we learn are at a fairly young age. They are learned when we are missing the full context which only appears as we grow up. The year was 1984 when eight young Girl Guides sat through a particular lesson in learning about trail signs and Warsha was one of those eight girls. They were told that at the end of the lesson they were to independently negotiate a small trail set on the school grounds by the instructor. Eager to show off their newly acquired skills they set off one after the other on the said trail.

The trail of course, had the signs marked for directions, a little activity set at each of the milestones, like taking a sip of water from the canteen (if they managed to find it, that is!), pick up a bit of rubbish from the 'forest' floor, etc. It turned out to be a comedy of errors and most of them arrived at their destination with varying degrees of success. Their instructor had a great sense of humour and made their return to the home base and debrief of the group's navigation a fun event. That wasn't the learning the instructor actually had in mind though.

After they were all back, the instructor put the group together as a team and had each identify their strengths in the trail navigation exercise, their assigned roles, including a leader. As a team they set off on the trail again and successfully finished it accurately and in time!

The instructor's words which defined teamwork still rings true for Warsha: "The strength of a fist is much stronger than that of an open palm." At that young age Warsha discovered the power of a balanced team: strengths, perspectives and cultures of team members working together to reach a common goal where courage, compassion, creativity and resourcefulness come shining through.

So, let's talk about how to bring this balanced team together. It begs a chicken or egg kind of question: if business is a team sport, which comes first – people or culture? The choice is either to select the right people for your team or to define a transparent and accountable teamwork culture before bringing people in to fit.

The answer to the question is quite clear from our experience. The seeds of the culture are sown first, from day one, by the founder. The culture is a product of the original transformational vision, values and ethics and its seeds are woven into the strategy, flowing into the team and each team member's journey from selection, inspiration and journey through to exit.

To paraphrase Jim Collins from his book, *Good to Great*, get the right seats on the bus, fill the seats with the right people and get them doing the right things.

Good to Great offers a high-level methodology to ensure that you have properly defined roles within your organisation and bring in the people who align with your organisation's culture. What is particularly important is the detailed description of each role's deliverables and KPIs so that you have a clear playing field and can move ahead together as a cohesive team. When you have this right, watch magic happen as a team functions together as a unit, leaning on each other's strengths, filling in the weaknesses, and members moving as one towards a single destination.

As Andrew Carnegie famously said: "Teamwork is the ability to work together toward a common vision. The ability to direct individual accomplishments toward organisational objectives. It is the fuel that allows common people to attain uncommon results."

While we are talking about getting an exceptional team together, it is important to also give a thought to your own leadership style. There isn't one without the other, you know. Nurture and develop your leadership style to lead these amazing people you are bringing together into the equally amazing culture.

In 2016 one of our coaching clients, let us call him Larry Cooper, took over the reins of the 25-year-old family firm established by his parents in the Middle East. The firm, while respected and recognised as one of the oldest firms in the sector, was stagnant and was struggling financially.

It was ripe for revival. His parents were preparing to retire and were looking forward to leaving the firm in the hands of their son. Entrepreneurial as they were, Larry's mum and dad were from a generation of business owners who ran their organisations the 'traditional way'. The way where the firm's organisational structure was rather vertical and the culture was based on a place of control. The 'get to work and do your job' kind of scenario.

Larry started his role in the family business from the shop floor and worked his way through to the boardroom over the course of three years. Straight after gaining his MBA and before joining his parents, Larry had worked with a startup for a short time. This company was a fast-paced consultancy with an open and transparent team culture at its heart. Here Larry had the opportunity to experience first-hand what it was like to be part of a highly motivated and engaged team. The founders of the startup spoke a different language from what he was used to hearing from his parents when talking about their business and their people.

Larry's interest in building a strong, people-oriented culture was sparked, and how!

Fast-forward to day one of him joining the family firm. Larry began noticing the difference in leadership styles and the effect it had on the people. Over the course of three years, he committed to the task of transforming the culture and defining his own leadership style.

During our coaching sessions we discussed and agreed on a few ways to achieve this. Because guess what? When your people grow, they grow the company with them.

- Be your people's friend, philosopher and guide.

- Be their CEO, coach and cheerleader with equal enthusiasm.

- Trust and respect them for what they bring to the table.

- Share their dreams, extend a hand to help them up and watch them grow.

The revival of the firm was on! In the four years since taking over the reins, he put the team's wellbeing and their development first. He worked hard to rebuild the trust and transparency in communication with his people. Larry's open and approachable manner made conversations at all levels easy.

As you would expect, the firm was going through a sea change. The team was coming together as one with renewed vigour and stood shoulder to shoulder with their new leader to bring the firm back to its feet. Larry is today recognised in the region as one of the best modern-day 'servant leaders' who built his leadership style on a few strongly held practices:

- Engage

- Empower

- Listen

- Ask

- Coach

- Care

How do you think he responds to the accolades? Yes, you guessed it. "I am privileged to work with the best team ever."

Element 4: Cashflow & Systems

Whether you like it or not, your systems are at the heart of your business and your cashflow is its life blood. Being informed and 'cashed up' is the name of the game here. While you may need, at a minimum, to be able to produce a set of audited financials for regulatory bodies or investors, you have the opportunity to consider getting more out of your systems and benefit from accurate, timely and relevant information to make better decisions. And by leveraging your systems you can improve the velocity of cash flowing through your business.

For many business owners the accounting system is a mystery, the point of sales system a useful but stand-alone platform to record sales, while an HR system to manage your team is often overlooked entirely. Your systems really are one of the least popular or 'sexy' areas of your business to work on and yet they are so much easier today than ever.

We talked about Evan's mother running her general trading store from the 1960s through to the mid-1980s. When we were writing this section, Evan recalled his mother having no systems other than cash, cash control, an adding machine for stocktake and a very manual ledger process (daybook) to create her accounts, employing very strong mental arithmetic skills which are less common today.

Anyway, because it was such a manual process the books were only closed every quarter. This included stocktaking of all her product ranges in the grocery and drapery section. She also had tailors working for her so she had to make estimates for the work in progress, taking into account the cost of clothing manufactured and sold. Imagine how much easier it would have been for her to run her business with today's technology!

Today, there is little excuse not to find the suitable systems you need on the cloud and have them all integrate and work seamlessly together. Moreover, most cloud-based platforms come with mobile apps that put tremendous power into your hands with timely information at your fingertips.

Why would we dwell on this point you may ask? You have strength in knowing your numbers so you can know where you are, always. Starting with knowing how much cash you have in your bank account and knowing who owes you money every day, through to drawing out and using 'management information' like KPIs in your daily operations, you can have a firmer handle on how you are travelling during each month. And by keeping your information systems simple (this is a 'KISS' variant we like to use) and up-to-date, it will mean you can close your monthly reporting cycle very quickly and keep looking forward in your business rather than dwell on what was.

To us, a month end close should really just be another day, likewise the end of year close.

If you keep on top of the information, you are keeping yourself informed and looking forward. We did a podcast some time back on 'how you drive your car' and how it compares to running your business. Ideally you look to the future through your windscreen at the road ahead using 'leading indicators' that help you trim your sails on the fly, and you use your rear-view mirrors to take in some 'lagging indicators' which provide useful information but are not the main game of looking forward.

Speaking of looking forward, do you have enough cash in your operational war chest to survive for at least three months if there is a hit to your sales? And this is particularly with reference to your fixed costs (or costs that are not directly linked to your revenue). Remember that business is always cyclical with peaks and troughs and being able to weather the storm with enough cash is a good tactical move for you to have in place. If it is possible, you should know what your employee benefit costs are and also have that cash put aside as a precaution.

If you have a budget in place already, great, if not, use a simple table, spreadsheet or an online accounting system to establish the level of cash you would need to make sure you can survive any bumps in the road ahead.

Ultimately everything in your business boils down to cash. Cash is cash (and king as is often said), while everything else is a journal entry. Your system helps make sense of the movement of cash through your business but using the information smartly will help you maximise the cash you have. In the most simplistic terms, it's not what you make, but rather what you keep and your systems are key to help make this happen for you. We'll take a deeper dive into this important aspect of your business in later chapters.

Element 5: Efficient Operations

Think of this in terms of building your perfect business to model and license out to other entrepreneurs (i.e. a franchise). For it to be effective you will need to replicate it effortlessly and produce 'same-same' for your new customers in your new locations. We want to measure twice and cut once in order to serve your customers while making it fun for your team at the same time.

To begin tightening the belt here you will need a powerful communication structure with your team. It could be as simple as a daily standup five-minute meeting with direct reports to share your day's priority and ask for help you may need through to a monthly sit-down meeting to review what went well and what could go better. This communication space is also used to cascade your vision and strategy down to the frontline team and thereby align the right effort towards the right goal with the right priority to meet the milestones in your mountain ascent.

To tweak your weekly performance and thus influence where your month will end up you could be reviewing your leading indicators, KPIs, to see how you are tracking and what pick-up is needed to meet targets. This is where your management system components will come into their own with tracking the important measures you need to keep an eye on. For some firms it would be seeing how many qualified leads you have in your pipeline through to a restaurant's bookings report for the evening meal and comparing these with historical pick-up rates to help assess how your business trend is progressing.

One of the key metaphors we will also talk about later on is finding any dripping taps in your business. There's nothing more irritating at night when you are trying to sleep, right? What is even more irritating is being presented with a large water bill and not knowing where the leak is!

So too in your business, it is important to look out and listen for places in the operation where there could be wasted resources or people issues. From reviewing your food waste in a restaurant, tracking your team's hours as compared to sales output or even conducting surprise stocktakes are all practices or procedures you could introduce to improve how your operation lifts its game over time.

Evan spent the better part of his corporate career in hospitality and often talks about his experience from the inner workings of this enormous industry which employs millions. In the hotel 'game', the rooms division is the 'shiniest' vertical whereas the food and beverage division is usually the hardest to manage and maintain in good profitability.

Now compare this with a stand-alone restaurant where it is even more challenging for the operation because overhead expenses like rent must also be met without the benefit of other revenue streams to help offset such costs.

Notwithstanding, it is a given to keep a very keen eye on your service and kitchen labour hours relative to expected guests or footfall and revenues. Less obvious would be your procurement process and how often you go out to tender with your suppliers. Unless you ask for the best price you will not necessarily get it. In a previous hotel Evan worked in, the procurement tender process regularly brought in anywhere up to 10% savings on an annualised basis.

Another story he remembers is of a restaurateur friend in Australia who besides being a great chef is a very smart businessman. He kept a keen eye on potential dripping taps therefore managed to run a profitable chain of restaurants. One of the practices in his restaurants was to install magnets over his food disposal bins to salvage silverware that might otherwise have been thrown out unintentionally.

The restaurateur credits the creative ideas to successfully close dripping taps to his team. So, remember to engage your people in meaningful conversation and together save the business a fortune.

One key aspect of closing a dripping tap idea is mapping your process flows. As a business tool this is one of the most important things you can do because it makes training your team easier and sets the standard that your team can follow, every time. It will give rise to consistent delivery to your customer and allow for flexing of your operation during your scaling process. A great way to get your team to follow the process is to make it fun, make it enjoyable and reward them for innovation. Peer recognition is also an excellent way to boost morale so make it a part of the company's culture. By recognising team members or departments as a whole for following and constantly refining processes as you build them, you will set yourself up for flexibility and a hassle-free growth.

A funny process story and lesson Evan and his siblings learned when growing up was the laundry process put in place by their mother.

When any of them brought in their laundry baskets it was their individual job to check pockets for contents before putting the clothes in for a wash. The primary purpose of this task was to check for paper tissues that may have been forgotten in a pocket which when in the washing machine would make a mess of the cycle. So far so good, yes?

Well, Evan and his siblings were less than diligent with the task at hand so their mum then updated this process to include a consequence if not followed. The self-appointed 'Checker of Pockets' (mum) established a right to salvage anything found in said pockets, including pocket money.

Aha! After a couple of pocket money losses and subsequent good-natured bargaining, the lesson of the story was learned by the children; be mindful of and stick to the process. Do have fun while you are at it!

Time to assess

When taking on coaching or peer group clients we go through an exhaustive set of questions based on the Five Elements to assess their SQ (Scalability Quotient). Here we have placed a few simplified versions of those for you to answer to assess where your business is at currently. Go on, give it a go.

- Where do you want your company to be in five years?

- How would your business model respond if your sales doubled in the next quarter?

- How clear is your growth roadmap for the three-to-five-year goal?

- Who are the star players in your team to shoulder the responsibility along with you?

- How strong are your company's cash position and systems?

- How congruent are your operations with your strategy?

If you don't fully know the answers to these questions, keep reading. If you feel there is some wiggle room to improve, keep reading.

Your operation is the engine room that delivers your product to your customer every day and is your business model inflow, if you will. The more efficient, the better your profitability in terms of cost, control and output. The clearer and more instilled your vision and direction with your frontline team, the more coherent the follow-through. The more rigorous your monitoring of KPIs and embracing of action-taking accountability company-wide, the quicker your acceleration.

There is more to business than simply a model to support an idea or an innovation and selling it. There is the very clear link that flows from your business model and strategy through to your people and systems to help deliver your operation to your customer, and each of these important pieces work in concert to produce the hum of rhythm in your business and give you that seemingly elusive, yet much sought after, consistent result.

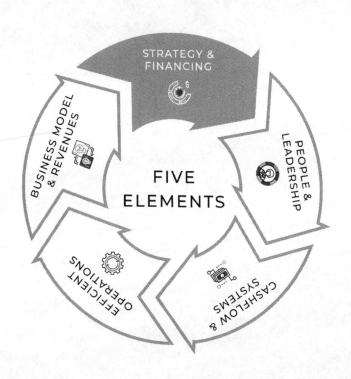

STRATEGY &
FINANCING

PEOPLE &
LEADERSHIP

FIVE
ELEMENTS

BUSINESS MODEL
& REVENUES

EFFICIENT
OPERATIONS

CASHFLOW &
SYSTEMS

CHAPTER 4

DARE TO SPEND TIME THINKING STRATEGICALLY

Connect your vision and 'why' with your strategy

We'd discussed how your personal story is linked to your transformational vision for your business and how it fires you up every day to get out there and do what you do. You are in a unique position of having a business vehicle through which you can make a difference in your world and make your vision come alive!

The challenge here always lies in bringing your vision all the way through to your customer and communicating it in a way that engages. The good news is the bridge between your vision, ethics and values and your customer lies soundly in your strategy and operation of your business model, so we know exactly where to start.

People usually buy from people they like and in the absence of having a personal relationship with a business owner they will buy from a place where they feel valued. How a customer establishes this rapport with you can vary a lot from person to person and yet the common thread is how your business walks the talk and delivers value above and beyond expectations. How that value is delivered is directly linked to the implementation of your strategy.

Warsha and Evan know we are not alone when we share the experience of being left totally gobsmacked when on the receiving end of very odd customer service.

We were in the market for a new motor vehicle and were 'doing the rounds' for a great deal during the summer a couple of years ago. At a dealership of a well-known brand, we were looking at their SUV offerings but had a peculiar interaction with the salesperson on duty. We were looking for a car for Warsha so she really was the 'MAN' (meaning, a person with the Means, Authority and Need) for the purchase, however the answer to each question she raised about the vehicle was given to Evan directly, without even so much as a glance at Warsha.

Evan directed the salesperson back to Warsha each time but that unaware salesperson who was determined to make the sale just couldn't take the hint. He continued to 'sell' to Evan and began assessing our income levels before we'd even come close to locking in a deal. We were far from being happy or closing a deal. Warsha went on to involve the floor manager who was equally dismissive and kept taking phone calls while we were talking to him. Needless to say, we walked away from that dealership and happily purchased another brand somewhere else.

Oh my, you can't make these things up! And what we experienced there is a breakdown of values cascading down through the team, along with a lack of establishing a rapport with the potential customer. The pity is that we as consumers often choose to let the matter rest and walk away so the business does not have an opportunity to rectify the situation, but instead loses a customer.

So, to learn from the mistakes of others, we come back to having fun connecting your 'why' to your vision, so we can develop your robust strategy that is appealing to your customer.

Strategy is a blueprint of your business

Warsha first met Imelda Dagus in 2011. Imelda and her husband Nick were based in the Middle East leading true-blue expatriate lifestyles, both with stable jobs. Something wasn't sitting right with Imelda though. She was looking for a future she could build for herself, a future with more than the 'nine to five', a future where she and her husband could make a real difference to their family, community, country and the world at large.

The entrepreneurial bug had bitten! In 2015 Imelda and Nick decided to return to the Philippines to start a business. Not knowing what form the business would take and after much soul-searching, Imelda discovered that the answer was closer than she ever thought. She decided to revive her grandmother's café! Granny's café business was a successful enterprise in the 1960s and was known for the great, locally sourced coffee and homemade pastries native to the region. In 2015 Imelda chose to carry the original founder's DNA forward and built the entire ethos around it. Her transformational vision is to continue the family legacy and to keep the Sulu coffee culture alive!

Imelda had spent most of her life as a corporate employee and stepping into entrepreneurship meant unlearning a lot in order to adapt, learn and practise a whole new way of life. She literally started from scratch.

It took a lot of courage to admit that she had a steep learning curve ahead of her and to ask for help. Knowing Imelda, we knew there was no dearth of courage! A life-long learner and go-getter, she immediately surrounded herself with a strong support system of mentors and peers to begin drawing up her business strategy. She believed strongly in building her strategy on strong family and community values, from preserving the local coffee culture, reviving dying traditions, helping the coffee farmers to providing employment to the youth in her city.

The journey, like it is for many new founders, was a bumpy ride which Imelda and Nick took complete control of. Today their successful coffee shop called Dennis Coffee Garden runs on a strong ethos of inclusivity and sustainability. Her dream of serving the locally grown and globally known coffee variety called Kahawa Sug and homemade native pastries is today a reality.

When we recently reconnected with Imelda we were struck by her progress. Her clarity in thinking through the strategy and converting that to efficient operations. Balancing her finances and creating an empowered culture through her company.

Your business strategy is the glue that holds it all together and gives fuel to your operations. It is the blueprint, the growth roadmap of your business. The second element of the foundation after your business model. It is the element which is shaped by your original transformational vision for your business. It is the big picture, the long-term view of your business, your path to the DARE-ing Milestone.

This big picture is formed by putting several pieces of the jigsaw puzzle together. These pieces are the details of the 'broad belts' of strategy and we are now poised to take a deep dive together into them. As we work our way through them, bear in mind that it is critical for you as a founder to train yourself into thinking strategically first and to then convert that strategy into action plans.

So, let us get down to it.

We talked previously about the broad belts of strategy: your Why, What, Who, Where, How and How Much.

Let's work on each of these to explore the various facets which make up the broad belts.

The Why

Your transformational vision

Andrew Carnegie talked in great depth with Napoleon Hill on the building blocks of his success. To him, like most ambitious entrepreneurs, the sport of business was about enjoying the work; it was also about winning. Wealth, prosperity or material riches were merely an outcome from the game.

Over the last decade or so, a great deal of emphasis has been placed upon finding your purpose or your 'why', upon loving what you do, do what you love and yet this is something Andrew Carnegie said nearly a century ago: "A man will always be more effective when engaged in the sort of work he likes best. That is why one's major purpose in life should be of his own choice. People who drift through life performing work they do not like, merely because they must have an income as a means of living, seldom get more than a living from their labour…"

Why do you do what you do is the simple question here. Surprisingly, the answer usually is equally simple, arising from our own life's lessons and experiences.

Values

You identified your top three values in Chapter 1. Core values, as you know, are the basic beliefs which you as a founder stand for, or the principles which shape your moral code. This in turn goes on to dictate your code of conduct. These values which the founder stands by shape the way the company does business.

Values become the guiding force for shaping the experience of all stakeholders associated with the company, all the way from the founder, the team, suppliers to the customers. Standing by your core values goes a long way to distilling the very essence of the company's distinct identity to set it apart from the crowds. By cascading into the company's culture, you are making it easier to continually inspire the team and to hold them together as one.

Four Seasons Hotels & Resorts which is now globally one of the most renowned luxury hotel brands, was founded in the early 1960s by Mr Isadore Sharp. As the founder and now Chairman of the organisation, Mr Sharp built the company's culture on his own values which he still holds dear. Inspired by the Four Seasons' 'Golden Rule', the company still operates on the unified central value of treating each other as you would like to be treated. Four Seasons as an organisation was voted amongst the Fortune 100 Best Places to Work for 23 years in a row and counting! Their corporate statement on 'How we behave' goes like this: "We demonstrate our beliefs most meaningfully in the way we treat each other and by the example we set for one another. In all our interactions with our guests, customers, business associates and colleagues, we seek to deal with others as we would have them deal with us."

Such an inspiration!

Ethics

Ethics and your core values go hand in hand and must evolve from the founder and their vision for shaping the organisation's culture. Remember that values are ideals to aspire to, whereas ethics are behaviours and conduct based on integrity.

Continuing with the story of Four Seasons Hotels & Resorts, here is what their corporate statement on their commitment to an ethical culture says: "Four Seasons is committed to conducting business in a manner that complies with applicable laws and is – and is perceived to be – consistent with the highest ethical standards, including standards intended to prevent bribery and corruption. Four Seasons is committed to understanding the risks that may compromise these standards and using all reasonable efforts to ensure that those who provide services to and for Four Seasons – including employees, contractors and agents – are aware of and share our commitment to an ethical and anti-bribery culture."

What is your statement on your company's ethics?

Place in the industry

Leading, going with the flow or follower. How do you see your company within your industry in the city, region or globally?

The legacy you wish to leave

It is important to put a thought towards the future of the business. You can scale it to sell, hand over to the next generation or run it until you are physically unable to or close it down. Whatever it is, be clear about it as this view of legacy affects the other belts in your strategy.

The transformation your product brings to the customer or end user

Now begins the customer-facing work. All products, whether physical or a service, are brought to market with a specific purpose in mind. This could be to fill a gap, to create a niche in the market or to elevate the offering compared to what is already available. Whatever the reason, one of the key factors to consider is how the product is bringing about a transformation in the customer's life. The discussion starts with answering simple questions like is it making life easier, better, simpler, saving time, money, effort? The more articulate the answer to this particular facet, the better your brand building and positioning will be.

While in the thinking and planning stages of her business, Imelda was clear on her answers. To her, the legacy she was reviving was of a strong leader in the city and region and as you already now know, the legacy she wishes to leave is one of supporting her community, her country and her planet.

The What

Defining your product

Macro and micro, both perspectives are necessary to be included while defining your product. Bear in mind that this facet and the previous one (transformation for your customer) are related to an extent. While the answer to this topic might appear fairly straightforward, we urge you to think from a zoomed-out view when describing the product by including the transformation it brings about.

Your brand development and placement

Knowing what your 'why' responses are, now is the time to bring them all together to describe in detail what your brand says, what the core vision is, what it stands for, what level it is in, basic, mid-level or premium in terms of offering. While going through this process, your brand consultants will walk you through refreshing your company's brand assets to now match the revised brand positioning.

Imelda said something which sums it up beautifully. She said: "Warsha, you agree that a good cup of coffee is made great by an inspiring story behind it, don't you?"

Remember what we had asked you a while ago. So, what is your story?

The long-term goal or your big, measurable milestone

There are several names and definitions for the long-term goals. North Star goals, 'reach for the stars' goals, 'big, hairy, audacious goal' (BHAG) as Jim Collins and Jerry Porras talked about in their book *Built to Last: Successful Habits of Visionary Companies*.

Or simply, 'DARE-ing Milestones' as we call it.

They all point to the big goals you aspire to achieve for your company. These goals are usually long-term for anywhere between five, 10 to 25 years! DARE-ing Milestones are meant to be big enough to be inspirational, to energise your people to join hands together to take the company forward. Imagine a mountaineer setting their sights on their Mount Everest. When thinking about the DARE-ing Milestone, remember that it must be guided by your company's transformational vision, values and ethics to truly resonate.

One of the famous milestones of all times is the one set by Bill Gates and Paul Allen when starting their 'little' company called Microsoft. They dreamt of putting a computer on every desk and in every home. Oh boy, has that dream become a reality!

Notice though that they were not alone and loosely worked with their 'peer group' which included hardware manufacturers to make this a reality.

One Phrase which drives operations

What is a one-phrase strategy (OPS)? As Verne Harnish famously said: "Underlying the brand promises you express is a 'one-phrase strategy' that drives your business model." An OPS is not a customer-facing brand promise. Rather, it supports delivering on your promises internally. Southwest Airlines' OPS is one of the world's most popular ones. Their 'Wheels Up' has driven every companywide decision in sync and is directed at keeping its planes in the air. Interestingly these phrases can change and evolve over time. Southwest originally worked with 'Meet customer's short-haul needs at fares competitive with the cost of automobile travel'.

The Who

Customer, culture, people, suppliers

The full development of your ideal customer starts with painting a picture of who your ideal or core customer is for whom you have built your product. Knowing who your core customer is will go a long way to creating your entire marketing strategy with sharp focus ensuring that the messaging is tailored for them.

'Speed, simplicity, and self-confidence.'

In the 1990s, Jack Welch, the legendary CEO of GE, lived by his mantra during his transformation of the organisation's culture. In those days it was in sharp contrast to the existing hierarchical and bureaucratic one he inherited.

The team culture within the company, the team itself and your suppliers/vendors are major stakeholders. Read on as we take a deep dive into this crucial part of the business further in the book.

The Where

Where are you based and where do you sell?

Identify your home market and the geographical region which forms the market for expansion. Find your niche, find your 'easiest to capture' core market where you match your customer's pain with your outcome so that you build your market share to emerge as the leader in the industry.

The How

How strong the bridge is between you as a company, your products and your customers is the topic of discussion here. The idea is to make it as easy as possible for your customers to find you, buy from you, return and refer you to others. Remember that if it is a physical product you offer, then make logistics and omni-channel marketing play a huge role in the ease of access.

The how goes back to how well you know who your core customers are and how well you have defined them which then leads to knowing where they are. Now that you know where to find them, make it easy for them to find you, whether online or offline. Imelda, in this scenario, will hardly be networking at a shipyard, for example.

Let us say you run a commercial bakery specialising in wedding cakes and your customers are wedding planners through whom you reach the end users, the bridal couple. You know you will 'speak' the language wedding planners speak, build your network with them while 'speaking' the language your end customer speaks.

So, ensure that your marketing activities are focused on getting your brand out and seen in the right places, the services are easily accessible to your core customers and make buying from you an easy process. Always double and triple check everything, be it the contact forms on your website to the signs leading to your office. Review all your collateral from an outsider's perspective. Review, refine, rinse, repeat.

The How Much

The old clichés are that 'cash is king', 'money makes the world go round' and above all 'having money gives you choices'. All are true, aren't they? As a pragmatic CFO Evan would regularly share with his team about this. After all, at some point, everything in your business will boil down to cash, so it does follow that this is an important pillar to your strategy and business and makes it worthy of close attention.

Two most common reasons why we believe businesses fail are the absence of a robust strategy and running out of cash.

Did you ever play Monopoly as a child? Well, we still enjoy playing it for it is a game of strategy, planning, taking calculated risks and yes, you are right, a game of managing your cash. If you ever played it or play it now, when does the game end for a player? The answer is quite simple, isn't it?

When the player runs out of cash, of course!

It is no different in a business. The 'how much' of funding your growth strategy and managing your operational cash are two key areas for you to master on your way to the summit.

We will delve into more details in a later chapter; however, you need to be aware of your key tactical levers as they relate to your 'how much' and operational cashflow. How you set your product pricing and how you accept payments are the two that apply to your inflows. Your inventory management and supplier payments are the two that apply to your outflows.

Managing these four areas closely and well will help you have adequate working cash on hand to run and grow your business.

An obvious and yet important comment to note here is it's best practice to keep your personal funds separate from your business. Just because there is cash in the business does not mean it's there to be 'borrowed' or is otherwise available to the owner. Have strict governance around this area and your business will thank you!

You need dedicated founder/CEO strategic thinking time

These days we are all busier and more 'connected' with our mobile devices than ever before. There are plenty of times Warsha and Evan feel totally overwhelmed and we find it necessary to step back and deliberately unplug so we can rest and recover to work more effectively 'on' our businesses. We would hazard a guess that we are not alone.

Why is this important you may ask?

To put this in perspective, consider this statement from an article Evan read a few years ago and one which he refers to often: "Today, now, this very moment, is the slowest pace of change you will experience in the rest of your life." (LinkedIn article by Fabian Diaz, 2017.) One of the tenets of the article noted that the pace of change for a company is linear whereas the pace of change for a consumer is exponential. Fast forward to now and that very rate of change has exploded. With this in mind it is easy to see that it is important for each of us, and in particular a business owner, to stop, breathe, look up and out to take in trends and then spend some quality thinking time on their business lest they find they get swept aside.

When Warsha takes on coaching clients, this is something she works on from the get-go. Almost eight times out of ten, these wonderful founders exclaim: "I spend all day and night thinking about my business. What do you mean put aside quiet time to think about it again?" During one such conversation, Warsha remembers the long session dedicated to helping the founder list and distinguish operational firefighting versus strategy pieces. The realisation which the founder eventually got to was that the strategy pieces were the ones rarely given the proper attention they needed which was indeed leading to long firefighting phases. Did we mention the 'stress ceiling' already?!

Quiet time is used to consider your strategy and how it links your vision through to your customer. Reflective time to consider the flow of your strategy and the milestones and capabilities you have in your plan. Leadership time to reflect on your team and the way forward. Thoughtful time to consider the needs of your customers and how to nurture them at a human level.

You will recall from our discussion on your support system that there are several places you can tap into for outside perspectives and help. In those very same places and particularly in a peer group you can carve out regular and dedicated time to work through your big challenges and ask for guidance for the tricky questions you might be facing. Focused time where you can put aside distractions like your mobile device with its (in our opinion) annoying notifications that are cleverly designed to interrupt and draw your attention away from what is important.

This reminds me of a fun game you can play the next time you go out to dinner. Everyone arrives and immediately puts their mobile device face down in the middle of the table, and preferably on silent please! The first person to reach for their phone pays for everyone's meal as a penalty.

Getting back to the point, it is important to wear your founder/CEO strategic thinking time hat regularly and consistently. Discipline is key here so start with small steps.

Let us walk you through Tariq Azim's story. Tariq runs a small department store and his busyness was raising his stress ceiling. Warsha walked him through the practice of putting together a routine for his thinking time. Tariq first started by being rigorous with his calendar management. He selected a day in his week, selected a time of that day and blocked an hour off for 'CEO Thinking Time'. This time now turned into a weekly recurring time slot. His Executive Assistant was brought into the picture to strictly guard (and enforce!) this time. She still does an excellent job of working all other meetings around this slot.

When Tariq sat down for this thinking time, the first week or two were extremely challenging especially as it was the first time he was doing something like this. He believed in the process and gave himself this time to just go over some of the old notes on his business strategy and appreciate the time to take a deep breath. This quiet time, even in those initial weeks, led to some brilliant 'AHA' moments for Tariq to apply immediately to his business. This thinking time has become non-negotiable for him due to the immense strides Tariq has made as a result of working diligently on his strategy.

Ah, those 'AHA's! Believe us, you will have a few when you sit down for your own thinking time. Like Tariq did, do resist the urge to stop the activity; remember that any new habit requires patience, persistence and practice to master.

We recommend using pen and paper. Yes, notebook and pen as opposed to an electronic screen to make notes. What you are doing is training your mind to think strategically and soon this notebook will become your constant companion for jotting down thoughts!

One of the tools we recommend you sit with (along with your notebook) is a 'DARE Strategy Map' which is inspired by the Strategy Cascade by Alan G. Lafley and Roger Martin from their book *Playing to Win*. The tool is designed to help you review and refine each aspect of your business's strategy, link them for clear next steps and circle back to the beginning. Much like 'lather, rinse, repeat', each shift in the market and each stage of scaling up is an opportunity to review your cascade.

Remember that business is a team sport and leveraging all your resources is the only way you will win in this game of games! The topmost resource which you are leveraging here is the sharpest of them all, your mind.

Know how to convert strategy into action

Knowing your strategy detail and how it is the blueprint of your business is great information on paper; however, it means very little if it is not applied and put into action. To action your strategy, you will need to feed your Why, Who, What, Where, How and How Much variables into your business model. Only then will you continue to solve your customer's pain points by delivering your product or service, thus generating revenues and you increasing your cash inflows.

The entire conversion of strategy (your thinking space) into action (your planning space) will need the collaboration of the functional heads in the business to break your DARE-ing Milestones down into bite-size annual chunks that in turn can be broken down into quarterly goals. A strong culture of accountability, which we have talked about, means planning can cascade into clear actions and have a role fully accountable for its successful delivery.

One of the practices Tariq put in place after a particularly successful thinking time was to bring together the functional heads in his business for a discussion, the objective being to establish an agreement framework on who was accountable for key metrics when chunking down their goals into bite-size and key milestones. Only then did they together cascade these high-level plans to their respective teams for quarterly, monthly and weekly goals. Tariq was determined to keep the team abreast of the details for them to be fully enrolled as an integral part of the drive.

The bite-size steps needed to be reviewed and referenced back to the strategy variables to ensure there was congruency in the vision for the strategy to operations plan. The detailed plan was then aggregated for the whole year to ensure that nothing had been omitted. Tariq was happy to have a plan in place to achieve all the milestones and was particularly pleased that there was a balance between his key and supporting priorities. .

Following Tariq's example, you are well on your way to meeting your annual targets that have been set!

Remember while you are in operations and delivery to customers, we often talk about the notion of a flywheel in your business as discussed by Jim Collins in his book *Good to Great*.

It took a lot of effort for Tariq to get his business moving and once he was up and running with the systems working in top shape, it took less effort to keep up the momentum. The focus always was to service his customers and get stuff done. To support the momentum, Tariq had his key metrics as leading indicators to help manage targets in a forward-looking manner rather than stopping to look over his shoulder at past performance only.

Points to remember:

- The biggest chunk to take away from this chapter is the absolute need for you, the founder, to first and foremost think strategically. A sound strategy leads to a strong scaling-up roadmap.

- Carve out strategic thinking time for your business. No distractions and ideally with a change in environment.

- This is where your support system would come into its own and where you can 'look up and look out' to engage with them to work through high-level matters facing your business. A peer group meeting is probably one of the best forums where you meet face to face (or online if applicable) and can leave your day-to-day behind you and be present with other like-minded folk and discuss your strategic concerns.

- Convert your strategy into operations. Chunk them into bite-size goals and effectively cascade them through the ranks. Keep the momentum going.

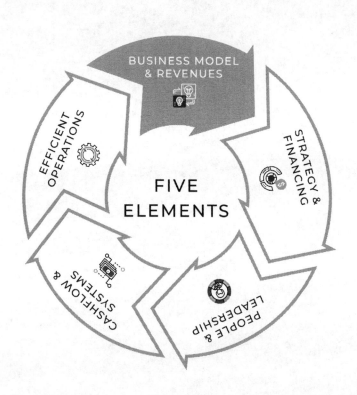

BUSINESS MODEL
& REVENUES

STRATEGY &
FINANCING

EFFICIENT
OPERATIONS

FIVE
ELEMENTS

CASHFLOW &
SYSTEMS

PEOPLE &
LEADERSHIP

CHAPTER 5

DARE TO REFINE YOUR BUSINESS MODEL

Remember that nothing happens until something is sold.

From a startup through to a mature company the truth is without sales and income the rest of our efforts on vision and strategic thinking, let alone people and operations planning, mean very little. If there is one thing that has come out of 2020 it's that everything can be up for review at a moment's notice, and reaching and continuing your relationship with your customers is always front and centre in both growing and challenged markets.

One of the examples which Evan talks about is of Hilti and how they refined their business model. This multinational giant caters to the construction, mining and infrastructure maintenance sectors by developing and manufacturing innovative products.

Hilti went on to disrupt their market by changing their business model from selling to a rental-based business model. There came a time when they realised that they could serve their customers' needs better by making the right tool available at the right time rather than making the tools available only for an outright purchase. Much like a car lease, in this model Hilti takes on the responsibility of maintaining the tools thereby providing flexibility to their customers to rent tools as and when needed thereby freeing up their cash.

Your business model and revenue generation form one of the key elements in the DARE methodology. This is because your business model is a distilled description of your economic engine, and while it draws on parts of your strategy and operations it needs to be very clear to you as the owner how it is you serve your customer to generate revenues. Think of it this way: your strategy is at a very high level at 40,000 feet; your operations are at ground level and your business model view is at about 5,000 feet. Detailed enough to see the moving parts and yet removed enough to take in market trends and outside influences.

As you move along your daring journey to scale your business, always remember to consider the best and most profitable way to serve your customer. Additionally, remember to lean on your leading indicators to see if anything might need tweaking in your engine room.

You need a compelling business proposition

Your business model and unique selling proposition is geared towards your customer. However, always consider the 'business proposition' of how you service your customer. Delivering on your clients' needs is always paramount but it should also make as much financial sense to you in how you service that need. It should be enjoyable and profitable and be helping you move towards your long-term goals lest you find yourself a 'commodity' in a highly competitive market with low margins and even lower barriers to entry.

So much of your success is contingent on the value you are providing to your customer. Remember this is so much more than features and benefits – it is how your product brings about transformation to your customer and it is something they consider well before the price. And in our experience, value always trumps price provided that value is clearly communicated in the first place.

The value can of course be something your customer cannot get anywhere else or it is done for them in a way that is hard to replicate.

In the production and manufacturing industries there is a concept or theory of constraints, usually called a bottleneck. There may be four or five main chokepoints in a process and a manufacturer would normally want to open up and increase the throughput of the tightest bottleneck first and thus increase efficiency. In your case you may want to see if you can identify and capitalise on such a chokepoint that could be unique to your market. It may be a tweak in your capability or simply innovating on some process that can be patented and thus makes it hard to replicate. Such a patent could even become a revenue stream for you under licensing fees.

We were working with James, an equipment manufacturer who supplies to several local market niches and had slowly gravitated towards supplying the medical industry. While there were a couple of products they fabricated, by and large they became a reseller of medical hardware because they did not have the economies of scale in the manufacturing space, no matter how constraints were re-examined.

When asked if there was any potential bottleneck they could own, James did say there was a persistent industry issue with certifying certain medical equipment as dry and germ-free after it had been washed. Admittedly there was an opportunity right there. To test this gap in the market, James redeployed some of his engineers and turned this resource into an internal thinktank to refresh their product line. This thinktank worked tirelessly over the next 12 months and presented some remarkable innovations to one of their existing products. After integrating, testing and validating this innovation, the product was repurposed for the healthcare market. Now here is the clincher. James and his team went on to register a patent for their innovation which was granted resulting in them now controlling the chokepoint in the industry.

With this move the company was able to make quantum leaps forward in their position as a global market leader and have already expanded their reach through key international reseller agreements. Sales, needless to say, have since exploded.

The main point here is the rest of the economic engine was essentially not changed, but by thinking strategically, elements were redirected to a higher margin product that was now able to be controlled through intellectual property.

Another good place we bring you back to is how your product brings transformation to your customer. There is a framework of questions we consider while looking at your core customer. The framework boils down to these four key questions:

- Who are they to you?

- Who are you to them?

- Why this?

- Why now?

The reason we would consider these is because it helps to keep customers' changing needs in front of you and to highlight what we might be able to do better. The more friction we remove from the customer journey and help them find you easily, the better their and your outcomes.

Let us talk a little about a couple we were coaching. Their business was online grocery delivery which was an emerging industry in the years before 2015. The regional psyche was still getting used to the whole idea, preferring to continue their supermarket visits as usual.

Well, what do you know? The milestone year 2020 dawned and along with it came the Covid-19 pandemic forcing people to remain indoors, more particularly at home.

Yes, you guessed it. All the marketing and tech development dollars certainly started paying dividends. Customers' shopping experience had changed forever.

Adaptability is key here. In the case of these businesses, they were ready for the change in the market. What they had to rapidly build up is the operational infrastructure to bear the massive weight of the exponential growth.

Productise your service

We find services to be a fascinating area to work with our clients. So often they will start at the generalist space and struggle with margins because they find themselves competing on the wrong thing: 'commodity' rather than value-adding service. The real value add for services is the little inclusions that are easy and often cheap to incorporate but have a high-value impact on the customer if you understand their pain points clearly. This also introduces a capability that you would be able to exploit and which sets you apart from your competitors.

Packaging your product allows you to simplify how you talk with your customer and lets you focus on the value and outcomes rather than fighting in a low-margin price war. Imagine how much more impact you will have in your community when you deploy a useful service that is ready-made and takes away your client's headache effortlessly.

Remember Dhiren and his company Cloudscape Technologies? They are a fine example in this case.

The IT industry can be very 'red ocean' with low barriers to entry for resellers and the space can get very crowded. Cloudscape Technologies found themselves in exactly this position when we started working with them. There was a lot of strategic work required to sharpen their market focus, but once the right customers and strategy were identified, the business model needed tweaking.

Dhiren is a great believer and advocate of productising services. As their forte was to work with stand-alone retail, their initial focus had been to provide a point of sales platform for sales, oh and by the way we also have accounting software you can use. Now, through a better understanding of the real pain point of the operators, Dhiren worked with his team to piece together the software components to productise the services into inventory management solutions. The team, now energised with this simplified structure and offering, were retrained to sell and deliver.

The results were amazing once they started speaking the right language to address the exact pain point of their customer, and adding annual after-sales care then became a breeze too. They haven't looked back since!

Another way to do this for pure service delivery is to have an SLA ('service level agreement') based contract where it is very clear from the outset exactly what the deliverable is, and by doing this 'scope creep' is dramatically reduced. The point of an SLA like this is to establish boundaries on your team's time and company profitability while ensuring that you can focus on what the customer needs rather than what they 'want'. Another benefit to both parties is you can focus on what you do best and uphold your market reputation as a leader.

From the operational point of view, you will be able to better understand and manage your resource allocations and product profitability. By productising you can work with and sell manageable chunks of your team's time and track relative efficiency through your dashboards. We will talk more about your labour KPIs in a later operations section.

A concluding note on packaging your service... do play to your strengths and don't give away the wrong thing. Rebecca, a client of our company Platinum VA, stopped our services because there was apparently a great new product in the market. One of our competitors began offering outsourced administrative assistance that also included a driver/delivery service (much like a 'concierge' company would). Initially Rebecca was thrilled but came to realise the services were not 'apple to apple'; she ended up coming back to us for admin services but retained only the driver service that she needed. Our competitor was first and foremost a concierge-like expert who could 'get things done' but was not geared up to provide high-quality executive assistance.

A great discovery by Platinum VA was to conduct pilot engagements to nut out the SLAs and establish what did and did not work. Additionally, it was a great way to learn how the client works and to nip little things in the bud early in the journey. Our takeaway is that the engagement is as much about how the client works with you as you work with them.

Do spare yourself the pain of having to learn costly lessons by understanding your customer's needs keenly and giving them what they need rather than want.

Balance your pricing and value you deliver

Balancing the pricing of your product mix versus the perceived value your customer is receiving can be very tricky to get right. Ideally you will have at least three products that you can sell in your product ladder: a 'core', a 'deluxe', and last but not least, a 'greasy burger'. By having a range of products at different price points you can get your customers to self-qualify into segments of your market and from there you can engage more effectively with them.

What we have noticed in the marketplace is potential clients seriously gravitate to 'greasy burgers' when cash gets tight. A client of ours, Yasmin, runs a human resource consultancy and normally didn't advertise that she would consider offering basic entry-level services. On an impulse she added the entry-level offering (a one-point SLA if you will) to her pricing page and at first very little came out of it.

Roll into 2020 and with the whole world's dynamics changing, she started to receive tons of interest and enquiries because many of her potential client team sizes were being downsized. Suddenly Yasmin was growing her customer base steadily once she had properly qualified the leads coming in.

An added bonus to this is around 25% of her 'greasy burger' clients have since opted for upgraded core services now that both parties have established a strong working relationship and the clients discovered that an outsourced solution worked extremely well for them in tight markets. On the other side of the spectrum, Yasmin discovered that a small percentage of her older clients were upgrading to her deluxe solution (which included strategic HR advice and planning) to leverage her experience with the leanness they were seeking in their restructuring efforts.

Bear in mind that the value you provide need not only be through your direct service delivery (which is expected to be amazing anyway!). By growing your customer base and thereby your list, remember there is always the potential to enhance your engagement with customers through social media, but more particularly by the email marketing channel. Leveraging email marketing will allow you to share tips and tricks, considered thought leadership opinions, share new products as they launch or bonus services like a podcast or blog. Remember too that you can run a drip campaign for potential clients to keep your touch points alive, and when they are ready will remember you and your services and reach out.

And as you are continuing your engagement with your customer base, it might be an idea to have a look at your customer lifetime values and where some of your best customers sit. Consider too asking them what their pain points are currently and seeking feedback on what has gone well and what could go better. The insights you get from loyal (or better yet, 'fan') customers is invaluable for a reality check on the value they receive and what they would continue to happily pay you.

Conduct a walk through your customer journey to ensure it is substantially error-free and frictionless. Potential customers should be able to find you and engage in dialogue with your company easily, and by having your team double-check your systems it will highlight any potential bottlenecks that might need addressing. Putting yourself in the shoes of your customer to better understand them and their journey is an invaluable tool to find any gaps or weaknesses in your processes in servicing your clients.

Be very clear about your core customer

It has been covered in several different ways already and yet the importance of knowing exactly who your core customer is cannot be stressed enough. There is a challenge, pain, problem or question they need answered and your solution ideally should be 'it'.

And being able to describe what your customer looks like (their 'persona'), where they spend their time away from the office, their hobbies and where they 'hang out' is a major part of being able to relate to and engage with these customers. With multiple products and ladders it may even be worth having a second persona identified. This is important because it will have a bearing on the language you employ in your marketing and how you narrow your search criteria for ideal prospects.

Having a clear idea of the persona you are seeking will help tremendously with disengaging with the wrong prospect early enough to avoid wasting each other's time. One thing is very important here and that is your customer acquisition cost. It might be worth recalculating exactly what your cost actually is and how it has moved in the last 12 and 24 months. If you are finding an increase in the cost it would be useful to know what has contributed to the increase in the event you might need to revisit your core customer definition.

Again, one of the many things that 2020 has taught most of us is that we can never take anything for granted, especially our core customer. A campaign of continuous engagement over social and email marketing channels again comes to the fore as a way of keeping in touch with your customer. With all the cleverness and access modern social media management platforms offer, social listening will help you keep an eye on customer sentiment trends. So too will tools like Google alerts help you with your trend monitoring and social platform monitoring efforts.

Points to remember:

- Arguably, examining your business model is the first step in scaling up your business. The combination of macro and micro elements of your customer delivery will help get clarity on how healthily your economic engine is humming along.

- Critically assessing potential bottlenecks will also help you be aware of where you might need to work before beginning your ascent on your mountain.

- Remembering that money will give you a means to meet your goals, it is timely to mention that the best businesses are profit aware, not necessarily profit driven. Being profit aware could stand in as a proxy for social responsibility because it means looking at metrics other than profit only.

- As a business you need to be making money while meeting your customers' needs. While it is extremely important to know the overall impact your business has had on your customers' lives and how they have managed to move forward, your business proposition and model needs to be sustainable.

- As part of your strategic thinking time, remember to review, refine and adapt your business model and revenue generation efforts to address changes in your ecosystem or advances in technology.

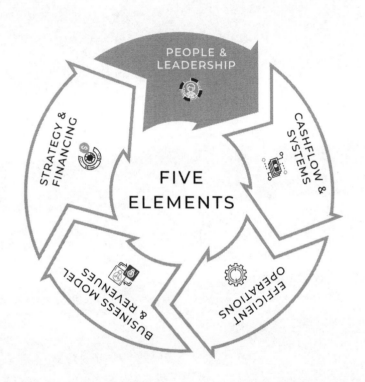

CHAPTER 6

DARE TO LEAD AN INSPIRED TEAM

You know, one of the strongest influences in Warsha's life has been her mother and her solid entrepreneurial mind.

As a young girl, Warsha saw her mother identifying opportunities in the market and starting her electroplating business. From humble beginnings operating out of a little shed the business was grown into a large, streamlined workshop with an excellent team working together. While Warsha's mother placed a great deal of importance on developing herself into a technical leader and keeping her finger on the industry's pulse, she placed even greater importance on developing herself as a leader for her people. More specifically, a fearless servant leader.

Becoming a servant leader was the first leadership lesson Warsha learned from her mother at the tender age of nine.

"Warsha," her mum said, "lead by example, look after your people, treat them with respect and inspire them to grow. They are the heart and soul of your company. They are the ones who are with you on this path. As a founder, your only job is to make sure that they are happy. They will in turn make sure that your customers are happy."

Over the years Warsha realised the immense impact the servant leadership lesson had on her and her ethos as a leader. The lesson has become one of the strongest guiding principles of her life as an entrepreneur and a coach.

An inspired team needs an inspired leader

Whenever you hear about an inspired business leader and their successful company, listen carefully and you will find that the company is filled with equally inspired people who are proud of what they do.

The truth is, an inspired team needs an inspired leader. An inspired leader brings together great people to nurture and develop them to be inspired leaders themselves.

You remember Larry? He built team relationships based on trust, respect, belief, love and compassion. The environment he crafted encouraged the team's healthy personal growth, allowed them to be intellectually challenged and brought them together to form a like-minded community. In turn the environment nurtured a sense of pride in everything the team did at both an individual and group level.

An inspired leader creates an empowered culture of transparency and accountability

Think back to a time when you interacted with someone who inspired you to do your best. In all probability you will find that that person genuinely demonstrated the values of a strong leader. They believed in your capabilities, respected and heard your opinions, trusted you to do your best, challenged and encouraged you to step out of your comfort zone. They genuinely wanted you to win, extended a helping hand whenever you needed, made you feel part of a community of winners and celebrated your every win, however big or small.

So why should it be any different in business? We talked about this culture earlier and the pillars it is built on. It starts with the vision, values and ethics of the founder. Like the Four Seasons story, their culture is built on the values of respect for and belief in its people, the same values as its founder, even after all these years.

When you learn to ride a horse, one of the first things you are taught is to build a partnership with your horse based on trust and respect for each other's intellect, capabilities and experience. Riding a horse is a fine balancing act, pun intended indeed! Once you are stable on the horse and progress through the stages, your coach will encourage you to loosen the reins a bit, to move with the horse and enjoy the ride!

Similarly, when you hire people for their culture fit, mindset, learning, skill and experience, place your trust in them and believe in their capabilities to do their job. Delegate properly and step back. Your only job at that stage is to nurture them, respect their perspectives, ask the right questions, then coach them to bring in the finer alignment to your organisation's way of doing things. Nurture them also to become inspired leaders in their own right to build their teams within their own departments.

While we talk in depth about being an inspiring leader, remember to 'walk the talk' by leading by example, giving strong direction and fearlessly taking decisive action – all essential in your own success as an effective leader.

A lovely story comes to mind. We call this story 'Leadership Lessons from Snow Runners'. We even recorded a podcast episode by the same name! The US state of Alaska holds a special place in our hearts and we have made it a point to visit a few times during winter, harsh as it is.

A few years ago, we went dog sledding (or mushing as it is known there) for the first time and while it was a thrilling experience, we walked away with a fascinating insight into the mechanics of the sport.

When we arrived at the location, we were first introduced to all the dogs in the kennels. And as most animals are, including us, humans, we all have our own personalities, our own capabilities, our own way of dealing with life, our own leadership style, and whether we admit it or not, our own place in the hierarchy of the pack.

Each dog is selected for the position they occupy in the formation, depending upon their personalities and place in the pack. The front ones are the leaders or the 'CEO' and 'Deputy CEO'. The pairs of dogs who follow fulfil various roles of picking up the direction (middle-management) to pulling the weight of the sled and being the 'wheels' or the runners (frontline teams). The musher or the 'driver' (the founder in the context of a business) takes up the rear and stands at the back of the sled, accountable for selecting their team (the dogs), providing the direction, taking quick and decisive action while navigating the tough terrain, controlling the speed or bringing the sled to a complete halt all by giving the commands (speaking) to the lead pair only who are all the way in the front.

We, sitting in the sled, were the 'customers' in this scenario. The half-hour journey was made quite entertaining and educational by the 'founder' as he explained the set-up.

Your strategy and business model are only as effective as the team and the team is only as effective as the leader.

Hire for culture fit and the rest will follow!

Fiercely protect your team and the team culture throughout the employee journey. Right from looking for candidates to fill a position, during the interview and selection process, induction to routine assessments all the way to exit interviews. In the conversations at the early stages, talk at length to get a deep understanding of their values, dreams and ambitions, what is their definition of success, what are some of the important things in life for them, their leadership style regardless of the level of the role you are looking to fill.

Broaden the interviewing process from an hour's worth of questions to a longer flow of conversation. Depending on the level being filled, have the second meeting over a meal. A lot can be read about a person when sharing a meal and this is so underutilised as an interview method. Perhaps even add a longer, third meeting on the 'factory floor' or in the office as a couple of hours of 'on the job' observation time. This is especially important if the role is supervisory at any level.

Your attention while on the skill set and experience must at all times be on the potential chemistry in a team culture fit scenario. After all, in today's fast-moving world skill sets require major upgrades every 10 years anyway so focusing on culture fit first makes complete sense.

Consider it as simple as making tea. You start by boiling water and then you start adding the various components to it depending on what sort of tea you are making and which culture that type of tea is from. Tea leaves, sugar, perhaps it is green tea leaves, oh wait, oh how about some spices like cloves, ginger or cardamom, then the milk… all these components bring their own texture, taste, colour, depth of flavour and richness to the water. When the right amount is added at the right time, they all blend in to form a fabulous cup of tea.

People of all behavioural styles make this world a weird and wonderful place to live in

The same is true for an organisation: it takes all behavioural styles to make a business work. When you begin building a team or begin assessing a team, it is important to have a balance in behavioural styles. While some styles are natural leaders, initiators, big picture thinkers, others are dedicated supporters, great at seeing projects through to completion, detail-oriented. While some are driven by tasks, others are driven by the team's energy; while some are the life of the party, others are great at being the dependable and caring friend. While some are super-fast-paced, others like to take their time to go through the tasks or conversations.

For example, when assembling a team to climb a mountain, along with your main team you will also need others like someone who stands back to view the full mountain and assess the easiest path to take (big picture), someone to check weather forecasts to plan the day's climb through to someone to keep track of where everyone is.

There are many great soft skills trainers who can spend some time with your team to assess each team member's behavioural style, and bring to their awareness how it works with other people. Your trainer can educate them on how to recognise and adapt to their fellow team members' styles and how the styles affect each individual's style of communication.

In our own company Platinum VA, we organise sessions at least once every quarter as a refresher to hone interpersonal skills for use within the team and with clients. This helps maintain the health and cohesiveness of the team and deepens their understanding of each other's ways of working, communication and problem-solving methods.

The impact on our team's performance over time has been impressive. From day one we focused first on culture fit (then upskilled as needed) with the firm belief that looking after the team's wellbeing has a flow-on effect to our clients. The major win for us was in 2020 when Platinum VA was recognised as the eighth best 'Great Place to Work' ™ in the entire Middle East, joining some bigger and better known brands in the top 10 list.

Have strong development assessment and plans in place for the team

Along with knowing 'who' they are, it is important to know 'what' they are good at and where there might be gaps in their skill set and what the plan is to develop them. We always say (and do), hire for culture fit first and you can always fill the gap in the skill set.

Measure the team's performance at least at every quarter end and encourage your team leaders to sit down for a discussion on the areas of development, be it in alignment to the values and culture or skill set. This ideally must lead to a development plan in conjunction with HR again followed up closely by the team leader in a series of coaching sessions.

Another area of assessment is to see who in the team brings their 'A' game to play, who brings the 'B' games and who, their 'C' games. This assessment is for both culture alignment and skill levels and the reason to assess this is to ensure that you nurture the superstar players, coach the middle orders and carry out a series of timed development conversations for the bottom end of the list for decisive action.

Remember, the more you entertain the calibre at the bottom end of the list, the more you are lowering the bar of inspiration for your superstar players.

As a leader, it is important to have the strength to take decisive action to preserve the integrity of the team and your ability to win.

Remember what we discussed earlier. Set the tone from the top, live the culture and lead by example. Create a healthy and nurturing space for your people to grow and watch as magic happens.

Have an honest 'table-top' which is open and transparent

If building relationships based on trust and respect are the roots of a great culture then transparency in communication is the water and fertiliser to nurture the relationship.

Set the tone from the top by sharing the strategic growth roadmap with the team, going into the details depending on the levels of roles within the organisation. Communicate the DARE-ing Milestones, the goals which are chunked down into bite-size achievable ones, the deliverables, KPIs and contribution of individual roles. Make understanding easy for all levels of roles perhaps by simplifying the language to something as visually clear as a traffic light reporting system.

Consistently communicate the progress, roadblocks and bottlenecks and encourage healthy discussions and debates to find ways to overcome them. Along with this, it is equally important to communicate your (in-)tolerance level of the lack of progress by putting a traffic light measurement in place. Ideally these also have consequences attached to each level which directly reflect back to the members of the team.

When the team knows that transparency is a value not only practised but held high within the organisation, the temptation to hold 'water cooler chats' doesn't even arise! Transparency in communication builds healthy teams, so give your people the freedom to play and win. Set your team up for success, coach them in their climb to the summit and celebrate their wins with them!

Hold and be held accountable

To err is human…

One of the things Warsha often says to her own team is to bear in mind that as humans, we will make mistakes. Instil the discipline to bring mistakes to your leader's attention so that it can be corrected, documented and learned from; it is about moving forward, not blame. What is important is how we stand up after the mistake. As a founder and leader, it is our role to have the backs of our team in the event of a mistake, especially if it has affected a customer.

You are accountable overall so take a minute and consider the difference in these two statements in response to a customer complaint:

- "This is OUR mistake and we will ensure that it is corrected so you get the full and positive experience as our customer. Thank you for your patience and for the continued business."

- "Yes, I know WHO in the department dropped the ball despite detailed instructions. I will make sure that they hear about it."

You already know which one is said by the leader who has their team's back! That's right, the first one.

A strongly built transparent culture shines through in the strategy, the brand, the team's engagement, product delivery, customer and vendor happiness, the achievements, celebrations and back into the long-term strategy.

Make your well-articulated vision, values and ethics a part of life in your workplace. Make it fun, remember to enjoy the journey together.

Every role contributes to company vision

We usually break out into a wide grin when we state the obvious! And yet each role does aggregate and contribute efficiently to the company vision if designed properly. There is however a subtlety in how roles work that can be very difficult to get right. When we consider this, the primary question to answer is what does the business need from each role?

Most businesses in our experience can boil down to four key functions whose heads report into the CEO. These areas are Operations, Marketing, Human Resources and Finance and the subtlety mentioned earlier is that they fit into an accountability chart with cross-functional dotted lines rather than a bog-standard and rigid corporate structure. It's not about title, it's all about what the business needs from the functions. And especially in the early days you may even find that one person could actually sit in two of these boxes and have multiple roles.

The trick is to step firmly into each of those roles and deliver on the accountability the business needs from that role rather than blur the edges between roles, confuse issues and become bogged down in overwhelm and disorder.

We've already talked at length about the CEO. That role is to set the company tone and direction, spend time thinking strategically, clearly communicate the vision and inspire and direct the function heads to deliver on their accountabilities. At times the CEO will need to be a mentor, at times a coach, but in all cases keeping the direction clear and heading for the next goals and DARE-ing Milestones.

For the four key functions you will need to get a little more granular and draw up a set of key skills that are needed to deliver on their accountabilities and only then you would go out to find suitable candidates with a strong culture fit to head them. In the meantime, this is where the CEO or other function head may also be covering one of these roles and where you need to be clear about what the company requires from the role.

This incidentally, as we talked about in the support system chapter, is another clear example of where individual egos need to be left at the door so we can remove any friction and get stuff done.

Once the key skills are identified for each function, you can then proceed to fully draw out the functional chart of each function. Again, it may be the case the roles are being covered by the function head, but it needs to be clear who should be doing what and when. With a bit more time, each functional role would be process mapped so that it becomes crystal clear how each role fits into the whole and therefore how each is delivering to the company vision.

Let's go back to Dhiren and his company Cloudscape Technologies. In its early stages Dhiren was wearing all the hats in the different functions and he was terribly overwhelmed not seeing the wood for the trees. One of the key needs that came to light very quickly in the coaching sessions was these functions needed to be delegated. Fortunately, Cloudscape Technologies was growing and the first of those hats to be delegated was marketing where Dhiren needed to bring in complementary strengths to help run that function. With the marketing role filled by the right person, next on the delegation list was the people (HR) function and then lastly the finance function was outsourced.

With the key support functions seen to, Dhiren as founder then only had two hats left which were the founder's strategic thinking hat and operations (IT technical head) overseeing the delivery team. With the renewed brain space now available to him, Dhiren was able to then begin working 'on' his business. The wonderful outcome was that Dhiren was then able to rest easier and develop his team, who in turn had clarity in their roles, in the deliverables and in how they fit into the bigger picture.

The rest is a little easier to manage and that starts with the cascading and breakdown of the overall strategy for each key function. What is critical here is to identify at least two key measurable KPIs (both leading and/or lagging as appropriate) that each key function would be aiming for and which can be communicated to the team in each function. From the CEO perspective you would assess these KPIs each week and month as you progress through your year and adjust the priority and focus as needed.

Let's lift up to the big picture view and take a look at the various functions. You will have noticed we deliberately use the term 'function' rather than verticals or silos. We do this so that we leave behind some less than ideal corporate practices and ideas that begin to take away from what the company needs. As flat a structure as can be managed is the aim that will allow for the right work to be done and yet will allow for efficient cooperation between the different functions. The objective is to get stuff done after all, and in that vein we are using our weekly and monthly

KPIs to assess how much we have all moved each month towards our annual and DARE-ing Milestones.

Points to remember:

- It is the people who are the heart and soul of your business. Look after them and they look after your customers. Create a place to let them be who they are and to enable them to grow into strong individuals.

- Always hire right for culture fit first to bring in the 'A' gamers who can unlearn and reskill easily enough to make for an empowered team.

- Give them a clear direction and enrolment into where the company is headed and they will understand exactly what part of the jigsaw they occupy in making the big picture come alive.

- And standing behind them all, the backbone to the operation, is you, the fearless founder and servant leader holding up a light to illuminate the path to success.

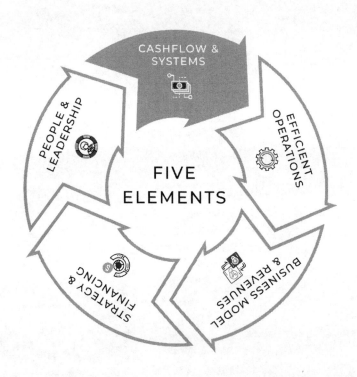

CHAPTER 7

DARE TO LEARN HOW FINANCE WORKS

You need a firm handle on working capital

The 'how much' we talked about earlier is centred on two key aspects: how you fund the growth of your business and how you manage your operational working capital. While business growth can be funded by capital injections (whether strategic equity or debt), in this book we are primarily considering your growth as being funded organically by your operations out of excess cash your business generates. The short of it is we are focused on your working capital management.

If you are not sure exactly what working capital is, the textbook definition is current assets in excess of current liabilities... (yeah, thanks for that!)... and all it really means is it's the cash running through your business to directly service your clients (i.e. your day-to-day cashflows which exclude 'investing' or 'long-term debt funding').

Current assets primarily include your cash in the bank, amounts your customers owe you and any inventory you have on hand. Accounts payable would normally be amounts you owe to your suppliers and monthly payroll for your team. It would of course follow that positive working capital (more assets than liabilities) is what you are after, but more importantly, you are specifically looking for fast conversion of non-cash items into cash.

Why fast conversion you may ask? Recall 'everything else is a journal entry' when we were talking about 'how much' in strategy? You can book (or account for) a ton of sales on account this month and your working capital looks great, but if it takes you 90 days to collect the cash then you will find yourself in a position of having to cover say three months of payroll before seeing the cash from sales. Probably not an ideal situation and one which requires you to have some cash reserves to draw on, hence the point of fast conversion of sales into cash.

There are four key areas that you need to be on top of to manage your existing working capital cycle effectively. Let's start by looking at the first two which affect your inflows in your accounts receivable: how you price your products and how you accept payments.

Inflow – Selling price

Setting the right price is key here. Your sales price is heavily biased towards what your market will pay but is also very firmly influenced by how you communicate the value you provide your customer. For example, packaging a service that is backed by outstanding attention to detail (something hard to put a direct price on) will work extremely well in this regard, and if you then take an additional step of backing it with a guaranteed service level you can 'productise' that service into an investment which makes it all the more valuable and even more compelling to your customer.

Remember the expression 'give an inch and they'll take a mile'? Most companies yield to meeting customers' 'wants' over and above their 'needs' and that can be a potential recipe for disaster. So, meet their needs and deliver it with a smile while working smarter as you continue to work hard. Do find time to create a product ladder with a 'greasy burger', core and deluxe levels of products so your customer can easily engage with you on all levels. And know your product profitability inside out so you can readily tell what your margins are and how best to work and promote your product mix.

Inflow – Cash collection

How you collect cash is arguably slightly more important than having the right price. Some bigger customers will use your terms to the full and be slow payers, so your pricing should take this into account. That said, how you nurture your relationships with customers goes a long way for them to pay more quickly. There are other strategies to draw on – you may want to consider deploying credit card collection which has a minimal cost but which also means you receive your money in days, not weeks or months.

Other ways are to offer discounts for early settlement or even to bill in advance or hold a deposit. Whatever method you choose to use, always look to avoid giving credit if you can but then monitor and chase outstanding amounts relentlessly if you do choose to offer credit. One other key lever here is you need to set accountability for accounts receivable; if this is not done it can be a very dangerous place to be if money is left in the market and not properly followed up.

Outflow – Inventory

If your business does not have inventory or a fabrication process in your delivery to customer, then read on. But if it does, then you will need to keep a close eye on it. For inventory, you are best served having an inventory system that ties into your point of sale or production system so you can dynamically know what your stock levels are. Reorder points and lead times need careful managing to ensure you are not holding too much stock at any point in time.

This is especially true for high-value/slow-moving stock, as it will tie up your available cash for too long. You may want to consider negotiating longer credit terms or sell on consignment (you only pay for stock when it is sold) if available. The other thing you might want to consider is to find ways to shorten your fabrication and customer delivery timeframes so you can get to the billing cycle more quickly.

Outflow – Suppliers

This leads on to the last of the areas and that is managing your supplier payments. Of course, you want to treat your suppliers with the same respect you do your customers so do pay on time. What you can do here is negotiate longer credit terms so that you have a chance to sell and collect cash before you need to pay your suppliers.

Your payroll disbursement is not specifically noted here because it is usually rigorously governed by legislation and is paid on a high priority; however, your key lever there is in your people management rather than actual payroll disbursement.

The key lesson on cashflow is it is not 'what you make' but 'what you keep' and moreover, the speed with which you can get the cash into your business. Remember that a cashflow statement is only a representation of how and where cash is running through your business and the important thing to activate is quick receipt and slower payments out. A key discipline that will serve you well is to keep a daily eye on both the cash in your bank account and who owes you money.

You need a strong cash pipeline to fund your growth

Strategic debt (bank or other borrowings)

We are not considering raising funds in this book, whether it is bank debt, overdrafts or funding rounds (equity). Our assumption is you're past the startup phase of your journey and are ready to grow organically, utilising your internally generated cash flows.

That said, there may well be times when you might need a strategic cash injection (over and above your reserve that we talk about in the next section) to tide you over. It is best to have your business take on the loan or overdraft directly – if your bank manager thinks your business can meet the payments then that is a good sign.

- If you put funds into the business yourself from your own savings, do treat it like debt and repay it at the earliest opportunity. Have your business pay for the privilege of using the funds (i.e. pays you interest) at least at a rate equivalent to what you have forgone with term deposits.

- We would never recommend taking out (additional) mortgages on assets the business does not own.

- We would absolutely not recommend taking out personal loans or credit card debt because the rates you will pay are too uneconomical, but if you do, be very careful and again, have your business pay you for the cost of borrowing and repay at the earliest opportunity.

We know you know and do remember that external debt will always come with interest and terms and conditions that have consequences. You never want to put yourself or your family at risk which is why we recommend your business take on the debt directly and under its own steam.

We recall a challenging situation when Ahmed Ali who ran a digital printing unit approached us for coaching. He had made a couple of poor cash decisions on the advice of a business partner who had since left the business. Ahmed had invested heavily in inventory and this had a knock-on effect on his payroll and payables. His bank would not lend any money and he had to put in his own cash from savings to top up the working capital. He soon discovered that that cash injection was not nearly enough so he had to go ahead and add a second mortgage to his house. Yikes!

Seeing his courage and determination to work his way out of this situation, we took him on as a client. Ahmed worked very hard over the next few months to sort out his working capital, especially his cash collection and inventory management, and slowly, slowly managed to right his ship. All the debts were repaid within 18 months! Despite the stress Ahmed experienced, his belief in himself and the tenacity to be able to salvage the situation saw him through. Kudos to him!

Cash from operations

When we looked at your inflow elements earlier, we only considered your 'as is' or existing process flow and the pieces you would need to look out for when managing your working capital. One very useful tip is to look at your sales process itself and see if you can make that lead time shorter and more efficient so as to increase your flow-through. In addition, you might want to consider increasing the size of your sales funnel itself… and this brings us to the growth aspect of your strategy and funding it.

Remember that we are only considering you growing your business organically and from internally generated cash. So, the constraint here, if any, is the flow-through of your sales/delivery/collection cycle to generate profit and excess cashflow that can be directed to your growth. Growth means you will need an increased amount of cash in your working capital available to hire more team members, increased levels of inventory and the like. And if you think about it carefully, this means you will need a strong and consistent flow of cash inflows to fund this growth.

Let's take a step back. Prudent cash management in your business would mean you would have already put aside three to six months' worth of cash outflows to be held as a reserve fund in the event there is either a slowing or uptick in business levels. A sudden drop in sales volume means you will need the cashflow runway to deal with adjusting your operations; and an uptick means you will need to be able to meet the increase in business levels which may include hiring more team members or increasing inventory levels.

Ideally you would already have a more detailed contingency plan developed with immediate actions that can be taken for unexpected business level changes.

Now, starting from your position of readiness with a cash reserve, we consider implementing your growth strategy. First and foremost, remember you will need to keep your eye on your big picture and head for your specific milestones. Consider that over a long distance a one-degree error off your course will have you end up in a very different place – so keeping your eye on the target is paramount and using your tools and metrics to keep that focus will help you manage the journey.

A good deal of thinking would have already taken place about how you are selling and implementing your strategy. So, as you shorten your sales cycle lead time and increase your sales volumes you are ramping up your capacity (and sometimes a specific capability) to meet and service the new volumes but you are also ensuring you are billing and collecting cash as quickly as you can. Do you notice you might be considering two metrics (KPIs) here: 'days outstanding' in your sales/receivables with another, possibly being a labour metric, which could be 'hours per income' or something complementary?

In the operations section we will talk a little more about key and sympathetic ('opposing' if you like) metrics that work together and give you a better feel for how you are progressing. Sometimes these are leading indicators (maybe qualified leads in your pipeline) and other times lagging (like 'days outstanding' which you can only know after the sale is made and cash actually collected). In any event you will need good information to properly understand where you are so you can make better and more timely decisions. For this kind of information, you will need a speedy information system, which in today's world includes robust business and accounting software.

Must have a robust reporting system

Your financial information is a key part of your business since it will record your performance (profit and loss), give you a picture of where you are (balance sheet) and how your operation boils down to your bank account balance (cashflow statement). Older cash-only or paper-based systems can work of course but information is less quickly available to you, so we would assume you have invested in a modern and robust electronic platform.

Recall that we talked about Evan's mum's business and the old-school, manual reporting system in place? Well, unsurprisingly, we continue to come across businesses which still run on pretty much reactive reporting. One such company, a family business, runs a trading company exporting consumer items primarily within the Middle East, and their customers are supermarkets. When Evan sat down for a mentoring session with a second-generation CEO some years back, he was rendered rather speechless when he learned that although their turnover was in the millions of dollars, the CEO still ran the entire operation manually, from live selling, deals, shipment ordering and receiving, all the way to closing the books each month.

The upside was the system worked very well; however, the downside was there were inherent risks to avoiding digital transformation. Working together it took 18 months to fully transition over to a cloud-based platform, update all the relevant processes and 'unlearn' the old and bed down the new with the team. The work was totally worth it for one simple fact: the timely availability of who owed money and being able to follow up quickly and radically improved cash receipts. Better yet, the windfall was the company was totally ready for VAT when it was announced in the UAE a year later!

With the multiple sales channels in the physical and online realms that are available today, you will need a central place to record your sales, receipts, payroll, disbursements or you will sink very quickly. And more than ever, a cloud-based platform is very affordable and accessible through a mobile app so you can have up-to-date information on the go. Throw in the ability to craft/record a budget and report against it and you now have some power at your fingertips.

But what is the use of a powerful system if you don't use it?

In days gone by, making a dashboard was often very laborious with manual spreadsheets but the apps today produce these for you on demand. Today, your system has all this information on the fly – from financial measures, daily cash balances (banks now interface account transactions directly into your system!), receivables, ageing analysis, sales reports and many more – so you are in a great position to be informed to make timely decisions. You would also be able to have a better handle on how your month is going to finish up without waiting for a long close of your books.

And speaking of this, you really want to aim to have your finance team close your books within two business days of each month. Evan speaks from experience here – the benefit is that your whole team is then looking forward sooner and anticipating the road ahead rather than behind and in the rear-view mirror.

Back to dashboards.

A specific kind of dashboard you may have heard of is a 'balanced scorecard' that you may want to consider using. But what should it show and how would you use it? The key premise of 'balanced' is that the report takes into consideration both financial and non-financial measures.

In the branded hotel game, there are four elements considered: financial (revenue, profit), people (team feedback, usually an annual survey), product (an annual brand standard audit) and customer score (based on after-stay surveys collated centrally by the brand). The report is collated monthly and its overarching purpose is for incentive bonuses.

The thinking is to focus the team's collective eyes on all aspects of the business rather than just profit which in the end will better align the operator and ownership interests. Likewise, you can easily introduce a balanced scorecard for your business and your cloud-based software will help you with information effortlessly.

Whether you use a balanced scorecard or not, at a minimum you need to know exactly what cash you have in your bank account on a daily basis and use the in built dashboards to keep yourself informed about your business, especially who owes you money.

Know how cash flows through your business

To reiterate an important takeaway... at some point everything in your business boils down to cash. Full stop. And like monopoly, if your cash is over, the game is over for sure.

The importance of your working capital cannot be overstated and your finance team should be able to provide you with weekly cashflow projections, and if they are not doing this for you, do insist. The balancing act of getting the money in, paying your people, growing and making enough to reinvest in the business is too important to leave to chance.

We take you back to Larry and his journey to change within his firm. You remember we said that the finance department required firm hand-holding, don't you? Well, one of the discoveries was of the state of their receivables and what was outstanding in the market. To Larry's shock he found out that the outstandings ran to the tune of nearly half a million dollars!

Larry put this point for discussion during the next coaching session and together we agreed to put this to the team as a theme for the quarter. Rather than make it just the finance department's job to collect the cash owed, the whole company came together to take on the task.

Every successful collection was cheered, the person bringing it in acknowledged, and before Larry knew it, the total collection for the quarter was nearly up to 80% of the total outstandings. The collections continued, the receivables process documentation was updated and rolled out successfully.

In the strategy section we mentioned the importance of separating your personal cash/finances from the business account. It is very well to remember you are treating your business as an adult and conducting your dealings at 'arm's length'. Do not 'borrow' from the company, ever. Instead, hold back at least 10%, or better 20%, of profit to reinvest in the business and then make a proper profit distribution per the profit share articles of your company and be done with it. Formalise reimbursement of company-related expenses where you use your personal credit card through expense claims that are properly signed off. These simple governance measures will help keep your books clean and will give you a true picture of your results.

If you make cash sales, be very aware of how the cash is controlled and banked. Ideally you will have a dedicated cashier that you can monitor and in any event your sales reports and cash collected should be 'audited' every day by someone independent in your finance team. If you let cash get out of your control you will, more often than not, end up with a terrible 'leaky tap' that is hard to identify and plug. Remember too that it need not be a large amount, but if regular enough it can cause you undue hardship.

We had a high-end baker as a client some years back and on the face of it they were doing very well. There were lots of cash sales along with the more regular card sales and yet the owner had a niggly feeling receipts were consistently down. Without going into detail, there was cash going missing and authorities had to be involved to address the issue which was estimated in the end to have cost about $10,000.

The moral of this story is to find your leaky taps and fix them at once!

It goes to show that the 'who' (in this case your team) matters as much, if not more, than your 'how much' and in all cases your engagement in the cashflow side of your business is too important to ignore. While you are thinking strategically on serving your customer it does bear spending some time understanding the inner workings too.

Points to remember:

- Work your four operational cashflow levers to maximise the cash in your business.

- Always know your cash balance and who owes you money.

- Set up your cash reserve ('rainy-day money') so you can cover three to six months of your operational costs if needed.

- Think carefully before bringing external debt into your business but manage it closely if you do.

- Utilise accounting and operational systems, dashboards and mobile apps to the full to ensure you have current information at your fingertips to make timely decisions.

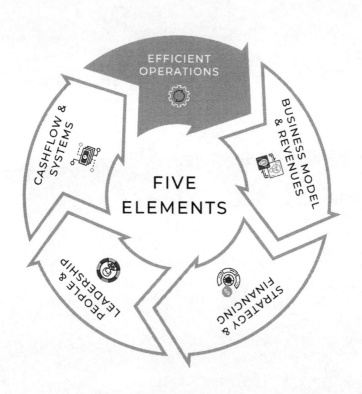

CHAPTER 8

DARE TO RUN EFFICIENT OPERATIONS

Strategy is all about thinking time for the big picture, thinking beyond the immediate, beyond six months at least.

Operations are all about planning a series of efficient actions to translate that strategic thinking time into action. Efficient operations require strong planning, disciplined routines, clear and transparent communication, clear role deliverables, measurable KPIs and organisational goals chunked down into quarterly (and monthly, weekly/daily goals as appropriate) targets for each role.

If your organisation has a strong customer base which turns over high revenues and yet finds it challenging to turn a profit, then it is time to investigate the operations plan for gaps, inefficient or ineffective resource utilisation.

You may find there is a leaky tap where cash is flowing out in droplets small enough to escape notice yet over time adds up to a considerable amount overall.

To put it simply, efficient operations enable the organisation to remain cost-effective while consistently delivering their product and their brand promise to their core customers.

We coach a founder, let us call her Elena Martin, who runs a decade-old firm. This firm manufactures professional uniforms for cabin crew, sports events, support staff and suchlike. While the top-line was great, when she came to us the company was struggling to maintain efficient floor management which included receiving the designs for the new orders, receiving fabric deliveries, workload allocations to tailors, quality control, packing and dispatch.

The two floor supervisors knew the loosely documented processes inside out and yet Elena and her senior team wanted to find a way to get the entire workforce to feel engaged, enrolled and taking ownership of their deliverables. The situation was unexpectedly brought to a head when the two floor supervisors moved on from the company and thus left the remaining floor team rudderless. The floor team continued working as best they all individually knew how and yet you can imagine the chaos that ensued without able supervision!

While on the face of it, it looks like the answer is simple and obvious, you will be surprised at just how many organisations lack a strongly built operational structure.

Over the three years that we have been working with Elena, yes, you guessed it right, together we took apart the various aspects of the company's leadership and floor operations to put them back together. Let us start with Elena and her team's unlearning curve, which was quite steep.

You have to break a few eggs to make an omelette, don't you?

Besides keeping the conversations going parallelly on the other four elements, the team's sleeves were rolled up for operational efficiency.

There are four major belts to efficient and immaculate operations: setting priorities, performance measurement, clear communications and defined processes.

Operational success is about setting and meeting the right priority

In the strategy section we talked about setting your DARE-ing Milestones which are your long-term, big goals. This is sometimes referred to as the big vision of the founder. Whatever it is called, the truth is that these DARE-ing Milestones need a plan to map out the path to achievement.

We find the usual reasons for missing clear goals set is messy operations leading to the team (from the founder to the frontline teams) being in the stressful firefighting mode. If you as a founder feel that you or your team are constantly busy yet log off for the day having achieved less than expected, then the first place to assess is the clarity of the existing growth roadmap and the clarity in communicating the deliverables and priority to the individual roles.

With the situation facing Elena, as with a lot of companies out there, it is this uncomfortable yet most crucial conversation which set the ball rolling for her company in bringing order to the chaos.

Why would it be uncomfortable, we hear you ask? Well, when the going is great, orders coming in, when you are riding a wave of success, you often slip into the mindset of 'why worry about fixing something which isn't broken'. It is easy to slip some elements of the business, which the founder or core members of the team are not good at, under the carpet. When the wave slows down, walking on this now lumpy carpet becomes that mirror which we avoid holding up to look into in case we see our own face!

Well, let us assume that the long-term or at least the mid-term roadmap is in place. Now is the time to sit down with your operations team to bring this goal and priority into smaller milestones, be it half-yearly, quarterly or even monthly milestones. This way, the tasks are simpler and easier to communicate to all levels within the teams. Remember, the smaller the chunks, the more detailed the task deliverables for each role so do take time for planning this roadmap.

This process of chunking the goal into smaller milestones has three strong benefits emerging. It helps to establish the correct KPIs and with a little bit of thought, the correct supporting metrics that work in tandem with your primary KPIs. By distilling down to your key KPIs, it will help enforce and prioritise the order of the activities to meet the milestones.

The right goals and performance measures align with the 'why' or the transformational vision of your company rather than just being about a dollar value. Remember that money is rarely a destination. It is merely a means to an end so the real goal is the 'why', because it is knowing what the bigger purpose of achieving something is which will keep the team inspired.

For Elena, this was a huge lesson. Since inception, the goals set for her company were, more often than not, financial goals only and the team had very little motivation, let alone an engaged, spirited level of inspiration in working together to achieve the results.

She realised that a dollar value to the revenue or profit is merely a short-sighted representation of success. It is what you plan to do with it that holds the human emotion together to drive result-oriented action. Truly moving DARE-ing Milestones, and all following milestones focus on the transformation for the customer, team, suppliers and founder rather than direct financial goals.

The question which helped Elena get the right priorities in place was simply: "What does earning that amount in profit allow you to do for your business, your team, and yourself?"

By asking the right question, Elena was able to shift her and the team's thinking around the goals and priorities. And with the clarity they were able to get some traction addressing the situation they had found themselves in.

Going back to DARE-ing Milestones, here are some examples for you to go through when working on your own long-term goals:

- Successfully deliver the brand promise standard of service to a certain number of clients over the next five years.

- Successfully attain a certain market share in your industry, city or region over the next five years.

- Successfully receive a certain number of referrals to become the most respected/referred name in the industry over the next five years.

Involve your team in the discussions about setting the DARE-ing Milestones and priorities to make them part of the achievement story right from the beginning. Only by encouraging full enrolment in the target-setting process will your team truly own them and thus engage in accountability for actions taken towards those goals.

Bear in mind a law of physics when setting your priorities: 'Every action has an equal and opposite reaction.' For every key priority you identify and set for your company, remember that there needs to be a supporting priority set to bring in the balance. Think of it like attempting to balance while standing on one leg. There is only so long you can do it without reaching out for support or lowering your other leg. Now visualise standing tall with feet shoulder width apart. Standing stable and strong on both feet.

Let us place this scenario in your business. If your key priority is to increase sales by 50% over the next two quarters without a supporting priority, then this is like standing on one leg. Now identify a supporting priority, in this case strengthening your operational infrastructure to smoothly handle influx of orders. How does it now feel? Immensely stable and strong, doesn't it? Remember to articulate both these priorities clearly along with their corresponding KPIs.

Measure your performance

'When performance is measured, performance improves. When performance is measured and reported back, the rate of improvement accelerates.' (Pearson's Law.)

This is particularly relevant for accountability reporting and Evan often quotes this law in two elements: Efficient Operations and People & Leadership. When we declare a target to an accountability group, it is absolutely OK for that group to check in on your progress and for you to report on it. By allowing yourself to be vulnerable, there is a very good chance you'll do what you say you will.

In the previous section, we introduced a notion of using the key and supporting priorities when you measure your progress. Find the ones that matter to you and your business and start reporting on them. Also look at your industry as there could be some measures that make total sense there and which you should adopt.

Remember from the finance section that your metrics should ideally never be purely financial. In addition, measures like total revenue, profit or even margin percent do not tell you much and are only available at the end of a reporting cycle anyway. These are lagging (looking to the past) indicators. What we really need is leading (forward-looking) indicators that give us better and more timely information to correct our course on the fly.

In the hotel game, revenue per available room, occupancy percent and average rate are combinations of financial and non-financial data. Because they are reported on a daily basis, they are both a leading (when used in the month) and lagging (final reported metric for the month) indicators. More importantly, if you look closely, there is a notion of perishable stock – if a room is not sold, it is lost for that day – and is a measure of capacity.

There is also business on the books (leading indicators) that feed into their yield systems which manage the prices released to the market. Airlines measure and yield their operations with a similar framework to hotels; however, they use language concerning seats, passengers, load factors, cash upgrades, loyalty point redemptions and revenue per mile. A shopping mall might track measures like footfall, rent per square foot or penetration rates. You get the idea.

The point here is to establish a measure or measures that matter to you. Pick those which are most important to look at daily, and what they tell you early enough is what you need to correct your course.

There are several other key metrics that you may want to measure. Consider the list here:

- Project progress measurement
- Specifics: e.g. number of sales, new hires, orders delivered, top line and bottom line, etc
- Customer satisfaction: NPS
- Employee satisfaction: eNPS
- Milestone achievement progress measurement

While focus is key in setting SMART goals and successfully achieving them, believing that goals stand alone is a myth. In the great balance of things, something's got to give. A solid roof does not stand on one support pillar alone; for strength and stability, it requires at least four equally strong pillars and that is a fact.

So, imagine that each goal set for growth is a support pillar. For example, if your goal or the smaller milestone is doubling your closed sales, then imagine what will happen when the inspired sales team achieves this significant milestone. With orders pouring in, if your operations are not built up to handle the incoming wave, the system will collapse with implications affecting every stakeholder. In this scenario, if strengthening the sales team is the first pillar then the supporting metric is strengthening the operational capabilities.

Clear, consistent and transparent communication

The usual corporate scenario is all about meetings, meetings and more meetings, isn't it? Evan still thinks about his years in large corporations and how more time was spent sitting in meetings to discuss or plan the things to do than having time to actually doing them! Oh, the stress times like these lead to!

Well, the best part of being the founder of a small to mid-sized organisation is that you have the power to take the decision on how you and your team utilise your time.

Communication touchpoints

For Elena the unlearning curve was to bring in a degree of discipline for herself and the entire team. Discipline for bringing about some predictable communication touchpoints.

The first of the comms touchpoints to be set up were the daily touchpoints. Some sectors like hotels, restaurants and supermarkets have made daily briefings an art form. These daily touchpoints or 'Dailies' are a great way to get everyone on the same page and yet few others have made them part of their routines.

You know by now that the tone is best set by the founder, so needless to say, Elena started with her immediate reports to get the Dailies in place.

Similar to the briefings, these meetings are standup touchpoint meetings to keep their tone brief, to the point and with a specific purpose. The primary objective of this touchpoint is to communicate the highlights of the attendees' individual work day, ideally no more than four points. They can include deliverables, wins and performance measurements.

Well, truth be told, what you would like these touchpoints to include depends on your company's priorities, measurements and individual roles.

For example, each participant ideally takes no more than 60 seconds in the Dailies. Yes, you read it right, 60 seconds, making the Dailies a brisk standup touchpoint which lasts less than 10 minutes. The team had better come prepared!

The purpose of the Dailies is sharing so everyone is on the same page. What they are not for are discussions of any kind. If you feel the need to ask questions, there may only be one and that too for clarity.

The mantra to remember in/during the Dailies is **DARE** (of course!):

Declare

All together

Rejoice

Exit

If you have never done this before, it can initially be quite a task to get your team into the comms touchpoints, to attend on time and come prepared. Start with small steps like the Dailies, lead by example, stay strong and watch them come together stronger than ever!

Elena and her team took nearly two weeks to get the Dailies in place for herself and her direct reports. When they did get into the cycle, the team surprised themselves on how just putting their deliverables in the 'open' was motivation enough to working on achieving them! Remember the peer groups we talked about earlier in the book? Well, that is exactly what the Dailies are, where the team has their peers holding each other accountable for the declarations, they are present to cheer each other on on their achievements and extend a helping hand when needed. When you are stating things on a daily basis, because it is in your and your peers' awareness, things are less likely to fall through the gaps.

Over a period of two months, each level of Elena's team had their own Dailies and the priorities filtered up when relevant, for immediate action. The Dailies changed the face of supervising in the organisation as each individual sat up because accountability had taken centre stage and they were getting things done!

Your comms touchpoints can be set according to your industry, sector and company's cultural needs. Dailies, 'Weeklies', 'Mid-Quarterlies', etc. It is important to bear in mind when setting up the comms touchpoints that the people participating are immediate or direct reports only and each individual comes prepared to share their inputs.

A great way to support the successful roll-out of the comms touchpoints is by making communication boards a norm. This is quite simply a whiteboard or a cork board which hangs in every work area or department, be it in finance, on the work floor or in the cafeteria, for everyone to view. This board is where you share the company's goals, milestones, priorities, deliverables, measurements, process highlights, etc. Remember, the more information you make available, the more included people feel. The more people feel included, the more they want to help each other win.

Speaking of wins, remember that the team that celebrates together stands strong together. Make celebrating wins, however big or small, a part of the team culture. Whether it is standing together to cheer the win, a celebratory pizza together or organising special evenings, make each win an occasion to remember.

Feed forward touchpoints

The second part of this component of setting up comms touchpoints is a 'Feed Forward' touchpoint with project teams upon completion of a project or each delivery cycle. Project debriefs are fairly common in most businesses.

What we have discovered is that while common, these meetings are also most tedious, making them the anticlimax of a successful completion or the stick in the face of a particularly challenging project. Teams usually have a love-hate relationship with project debriefs, as the meetings, if everyone does not keep the learning hat firmly on their heads (learning perspective, egoless), can quickly turn into a 'where did we go wrong?' or worse, 'which department is to blame?' conversation.

A better way to ensure that the theme of this touchpoint stays on point is to centre the entire debrief on two questions and two questions only:

- What went well?

- What could go better next time?

It also serves well to reiterate that egos should be left at the door. As with coaching and peer groups, it's about the process and sharing observations for a collective learning and way forward. The minute any of us fall into the 'blame game' trap, the conversation is over.

Evan remembers a little anecdote his grandmother repeatedly said: "You cannot argue with a liar." Why it resonates here is because when interacting with an ego you get a similar result: lots of reasons, excuses and answers for everything that deflect away from any bruising to the ego and that is the essence of the 'blame game'. So, once again, leaving egos at the door is a fundamental ingredient to powerful Feeding Forward touchpoints.

These questions encourage open conversation from the project's perspective, creativity on how things or tasks could be handled better, leading to creating, recreating or refining process flowcharts and cohesiveness among the team to build that all-important camaraderie.

Clearly defined processes lead to efficiency

People or process dependent are the two distinct methods of building your company's operations. Let us discuss the basic differences in the two to better understand both the concepts. Bear in mind that both methods bring their own limitations and restrictions so this discussion is not about a right or a wrong but more about fully grasping the pros and those limitations. This is in order to bring together the best of both worlds for a robust operational efficiency in an organisation starting its scaling up journey.

People dependent

Operations built on a foundation of dependence on its people is most often seen in new businesses, small businesses, some family businesses and sometimes even mid-sized businesses. The operations rely on the skills, capabilities and experiences of a handful of star performers from within the team.

Most family businesses in some parts of the world are built on loyal employees who bring in their experience gained over a period of time. There is great value for any organisation in having the strength of experience and loyalty of its people.

This scenario also poses a risk for the overall scalability of the company. Businesses built solely on a people dependency, we have noticed, are fairly vertical/hierarchical in their organisational structure, which translates to decision making, smallest to the most critical, dependent on the founder themselves, regardless of the age of the company. This bureaucratic method adds to the length of a process thereby leading to delayed action.

Inducting a new team member is a lengthier process as it requires a lot of learning on the job and hand-holding by the star performers. The risk of this scenario also is where, in the absence of these star performers, the operations departments see work piling up or the rest of the team needing to scramble to get the job done or even coming to a grinding halt.

Process dependent

Operations built on a foundation of dependence on its processes is most often taken up as an organisation begins its scaling up journey. Here, the operations rely on the standardised processes which convey the company's distinct way of doing things in alignment with its strategy, especially its brand promise, unique customer experience, etc.

When these processes are built, refined and perfected to an art form, many organisations go the extra mile to patent these processes to legally protect their intellectual property – essentially memorialising and cascading the founder's DNA.

In a company which is truly process-driven, the organisational structure is fairly flat where a second or third level of leaders is developed from within the team. These levels of leaders are grown in a culture of strong accountability with an equally strong corporate governance and delegation of authority where they are empowered to make decisions appropriate to each level. Job gets done and work continues.

Inducting a new member of the team is faster due to the availability of documentation to learn from allowing the hand-holding to be infinitely more efficient. Loss of a team member does not have an impact to the degree of the people-dependent company.

Be aware though that in a bid to bring efficiency, sole dependence on processes runs the risk of removing the personal touch to the service or product delivery. It could also bring people into a rather rigid mindset which resists adaptability when the market goes through its cycles of change.

Building a process within a department's functions requires a lot of inputs from each member of the team in that department and the departments it functions with. Process writing requires a lot of time and patience and attention to continuously test and refine each step. When done though, it is one of the most rewarding things your team and you would have done for the stability of the company.

Think back to Elena's story for a moment where her troubles started with two of her star performers, who were her supervisors, leaving. The hard truth hit home. These star performers controlled the workflow and had the greatest inputs to the day-to-day functioning.

These roles they played and the manner in which they undertook the functioning was all undocumented, residing in their minds. When they left, the company lost the intelligence or the intellectual property. A brain-drain of corporate knowledge indeed.

This meant restarting the day-to-day operational learning curve all over again by pulling in an 'all hands on deck mode' which gave Elena and the team quite a few sleepless nights. The 10 years of experience coming crashing down in a span of a few days.

What they cleverly did was choose the option of bringing both the methods of operational efficiency together as one melded culture. Elena stood strong and rallied her people to bring the company back to its feet.

Working tirelessly, the team, led by their fearless leader, took the bull by the horns and turned the entire stressful period into a learning experience. They began by identifying the critical processes which defined their company's DNA, and documenting the workflow, the description of the various roles, the people accountable and the people responsible.

They wrote processes for the functioning of almost every department:

- Founder/CEO's office
- Sales
- Designing
- Supply chain
- Manufacturing
- Quality control
- Packing
- Logistics
- Finance
- Human Resources

What helped them was to take a simplistic view of things. The best way for the team to do this was by just listing what they each did and bringing it to the process update meetings for review and then blending these with the master document which was being populated by their line team leader. As they wrote, they tested the processes for gaps, repetitions, decision making, document templates and overall efficiency to name a few elements.

Could they have brought in a consultant to take on this project? Of course. And yet, they chose not to. By involving each member of the team, they brought a sense of ownership and pride to their individual roles. They came together like never before.

It took them two years to come to a position of strength after being caught in the middle of a storm. Winners they all were as each member of those departments played a role in strengthening the company for the future.

Did they sit back after this massive achievement? Well, celebrated, yes, and continued to ensure the continuity of everything they had worked hard for. Even today, they assess the process every six months for potential for refinement to ensure they are kept up-to-date.

A success story for the books indeed!

Points to remember:

- Identify the key and supporting priorities along with their KPIs

- Identify the critical processes which define your company's DNA

- Roll out the comms touchpoints starting with the Dailies

- Inspire and unite your people to take this up as a competitive challenge

- Celebrate the success

- Continue to refine

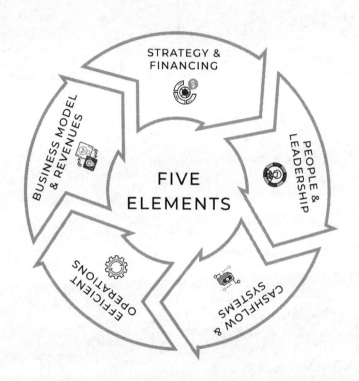

CHAPTER 9

DARE TO REVIEW REGULARLY

Over to you (or... The Beginning!)

Starting a business requires courage from the get-go. Seeing it through from startup to scale up requires tenacity. Taking a daring decision to scale it up to the next level, a boldness and an unwavering belief in yourself and the team around you. Congratulations!

Having worked your way through the ideas and methodologies of this book you are in a great position to firm up your vision, assess where you are and what might need change, begin your implementation, but above all, take action.

Be clear about what scaling up means to you

The beginning of everything, your scaling up journey included, begins with your goal, your intrepid DARE-ing

Milestone. A direction and reason so very strong that it will keep you excited and motivated through the challenging journey ahead. Ideally you would have imagined your three- to five-year DARE-ing Milestone to aim for along the way so you can stay on course to the goal that matters.

If you have not yet done it, imagine yourself in five years looking back at where you are now and get a sense of your feeling of excitement and accomplishment having reached the goals that you had set all those years ago. Know deep down that you have achieved it already and now all that is left is to do it.

Only you can truly hold the course by setting the direction and tone, and by steadfast and sometimes dogged determination to lead your team up your mountain. Starting from where you are now, have faith you will transform into the leader you need to become as you begin your quest. Even if it is really bumpy along the way, stay the course!

Like Admiral Stockdale said: "You must never confuse faith that you will prevail in the end – which you can never afford to lose – with the discipline to confront the most brutal facts of your current reality, whatever they might be."

And speaking about your future self, what words of encouragement would you think you would say to yourself in the here and now? We imagine you would tell yourself to stick with it, to see it through and that the secrets will be revealed to you as you grow. You may even tell yourself to start taking time out to do some real thinking or to stop 'sweating the petty things'.

The mechanics of 'how to' you already know: break the goals down into bite-size annual, quarterly and monthly goals, cascade it down to the team(s) and create functional accountabilities by role. Set your priorities and establish a regular communication cycle. Enrol your team in the goal-setting process and empower them to pick up the ball and run with it. Remember that business is a team sport, inside and outside of the company, and will require the congruent efforts of everyone to get you to your targets, both financial and non-financial.

And even if you know the 'how to', everyone's 'why' will be different. Consider the founders' stories you read throughout the book and how they scaled forward starting with their 'why', built or reset their businesses' foundations and claimed their dreams.

Look forward with anticipation to the first time you will be able to take three months off and have your business grow and thrive while you are away. I beg your pardon? Yes, take three months off. It is a worthwhile goal because it will mean for sure that you have a solid business in place and it is 'doing its thing' like it should. It is a vehicle to help you achieve your personal goals after all.

Here's an interesting thought. Have you considered that you are presently living the dreams of your former self?

What we imagine you are shooting for now is to live the dreams of your future self – maybe that is what scaling up might mean to you? – and in this context, is the point of going through your scaling journey.

Remember that three months off may not be your cup of tea but do pick some challenging personal goal that is worth going after and achieving – for you. No one else. You.

You must begin implementing

To get to your three months off though, you need to begin implementing. Focus on one thing at a time – implement, bed it down, review, tweak – and slowly and ever so surely (read as permanently) make the institutional improvements you need to draw you towards your vision.

We talked about setting the tone. Leading from the front. One of the first pieces that needs to be rolled out is accountability and your enrolment in the process is going to be watched very closely. When communicating why this is important, be absolutely clear that we are talking about the distinction between authority and responsibility. What this means is we delegate the authority to act and therefore insist on accountability for actions taken by the team. Ultimate responsibility rests with you of course, but be clear that we are not delegating responsibility which leads us to the 'blame game'. Remember to leave your ego at the door and begin being accountable in front of your team. It will make the world of difference and set you on the right footing from the get-go.

Remember though, change will not come easily for most of your team. It will take some time to get your team aligned and persist in the efforts. Even if you are starting with your communication touchpoints, the key is to be transparent and direct. Remove fat and vague language from your vocabulary and hold your team to what they say and how they say it. Encourage your team daily, acknowledge and celebrate wins and make it fun. No fun, no good.

Consider having a quarterly theme for your implementation efforts. Give the team something to get behind or involved with. Maybe consider making teams that compete for a prize at your quarterly celebration. Do something that will make it easy to be consistent with your message and so the learning being ingrained with the team sticks for the long term. Recall that most people are motivated by recognition and this will make such a difference within your team when you discover this secret for yourself.

Remember Larry? He was having trouble with where to start with his quest for bringing about change in the firm which he inherited. Finance and receivables were areas which required steady hand-holding. Consistent training was needed and product delivery was tired and required a complete overhaul. Communication in the company was non-existent and departments worked in silos. HR did not exist as a department. The issue was that as a second-generation CEO he inherited a system that was no longer working in the modern age, so he was stuck with what to do next and needed to get out of the weeds and step back to see the wood for the trees. It took us some time.

The place to start was in his own leadership development and the communications space. It was such a transformational change that took the team, the company and market by storm. Kudos to Larry for believing in himself, the team and the company as he, against all odds, continued to adapt.

Assess for success (analyse)

Now that you are on your way it gets easier. Assess what is happening and remember to focus on one change at a time. Think of the spinning plate image. Start with one and as you have it spinning properly, introduce the next one while maintaining the first. After another couple you should have your first follower stepping in to help keep the first couple of plates turning while you continue adding more. The wonderful news is you'll eventually get to leave the plates as they will spin themselves because your team will have learned the lessons and will be unconsciously applying them. Bravo!

Leverage your KPIs and supporting metrics. Remember Pearson's Law – when you report on measurement your rate of improvement accelerates; the more you insist on tracking your gains and celebrating your wins, the more engaged your team and your overall rate of acceleration will sky rocket to a 'new normal'.

Measure twice, cut once is a favourite expression and way to be for a carpenter. So too for your journey – make sure you have the right metrics, accurately measured, so you can make informed decisions in a timely manner. Correcting for a one-degree deviation off course after one week is so much easier to do than to attempt a course correction after six months.

Dare to take action

We dare you to take action. Stand up and be counted. You didn't come this far to only come this far. Dare to take your decision to scale up and dare to take the necessary steps to move forward.

Get your support system in place. Leverage all the experience around you.

Inspire your team and your customers. Share your dreams. Share your human side, your strengths and vulnerabilities (yes!) and immerse them in the dream you are building together. Involve them as you transform their lives and you become an industry leader in your own right.

And while you are doing all this, notice how your own life is transforming. How you are able to spend more time with your family and keeping yourself in shape. Enjoying your hobbies and participating in your sports. Engaging with and saying yes to the things your future self sees as important and worthwhile.

You read about some courageous entrepreneurs.

Imelda dared to build her strategy based on the values her grandmother had left as a legacy and she stands strong as one of the inspiring leaders in her community. Supporting every member of the supply chain from farmer to consumer and keeping traditions alive.

Larry dared to change the traditional management style in the business he inherited and today leads a thriving business fit for the 21st century. Believing in his people, encouraging them to dream big, empowering them to be achievers in their own right.

Elena dared to rebuild her company's operations and bring them to today's flawless process-driven delivery. Constantly refining, constantly improving, constantly striving for excellence.

Dhiren dared to start his entrepreneurial journey with an open mind to unlearn, prepare and implement a brilliant strategy. A business built from the ground up. Dhiren is now scaling a modern tech business with aspirations of going global.

We wrote this book with a view to helping you and to bring like-minded people together to create an ecosystem to make available the help, guidance and support to nurture entrepreneurship. We wrote this book for the courageous business owner, entrepreneur, founder, you.

So today dare to believe in your dreams, dare to take action, dare to inspire, because the truth is your vision IS achievable for YOU. Let's do this!

Keep growing.

Becoming.

Living your dreams.

About the Authors

Warsha Joshi

A business coach with hands-on business experience is an exclusive club and one to which Warsha certainly belongs.

Warsha is driven by a relentless passion for enabling entrepreneurs to achieve their goals, especially second-generation CEOs of family-run businesses. Today she is a much sought-after business scaling up coach for the SME segment as well as a facilitator for strategic planning sessions. She, along with her husband Evan, runs their exclusive Scalability Quotient Acceleration and Elevation programmes. Warsha is also a Master Practitioner of NLP, professional certified mBit Coach.

Warsha began her entrepreneurial journey in the mid-1980s in India where she started, successfully scaled and sold two businesses. She is also the founder and pioneer of virtual business support services in the region through her company Platinum VA.

Warsha loves living in the dynamic city of Dubai with Evan and their three cats. Her treasured moments are when she is at the stable looking after and riding her two horses.

https://www.linkedin.com/in/warshajoshi/
https://daretoscale.com/

Evan Le Clus

Senior corporate executive turned entrepreneur and CFO mentor, he brings his own style and experience to his mentees.

Evan gained his experience as a corporate finance professional of nearly 30 years with multinationals in varied industries such as hospitality, private equity and theme parks. CPA and commerce graduate, Evan is a hands-on business mentor for SME founders looking to take their businesses to the next level. He coaches entrepreneurs to resolve internal conflicts, make aligned decisions and take action by leveraging his skills as a Master Practitioner of NLP and an mBit coach. Together with his wife Warsha, Evan runs their exclusive Scalability Quotient Acceleration and Elevation programmes.

The dynamic leadership of Dubai where he resides with Warsha, their three cats and two horses, is a constant source of inspiration. He loves a round of golf, scuba diving, good books, thought-provoking cinema, and the company of good friends.

https://www.linkedin.com/in/evanleclus/

https://daretoscale.com/

Testimonials

'Concise and sound advice for any SME to have the courage to take that next step.'

Joseph Margow, Private Equity Industry Expert
Australia

'…evolve from a founder to a servant leader… if you want to scale this is for you.'

Rajiv Handa, Managing Partner, Bizlocity Enablers
India

'This book teaches you the foundational blocks of knowledge that every entrepreneur should be taught. Enough said.'

Dhiren Bhatia, CEO, Cloudscape Technologies
United Arab Emirates

'This book is a clear map to scale up confidently.'

Imelda Dagus, CEO, Dennis Coffee Garden
Philippines